Artificial Intelligence
PROMISE AND PERFORMANCE

to Ula

Artificial Intelligence
PROMISE AND PERFORMANCE

ALAIN BONNET

Professeur, l'Ecole Nationale Supérieure des Télécommunications, Paris

Preface by
JACQUES PITRAT

Translated by
JACK HOWLETT

Prentice/Hall PHI International

Englewood Cliffs, N.J. London Mexico New Delhi Rio de Janeiro
Singapore Sydney Tokyo Toronto Wellington

The original edition of this work was published in France by InterÉditions, Paris, under the title L'intelligence artificielle: Promesses et Réalités, © 1984 by InterÉditions.

Library of Congress Cataloging-in-Publication Data

Bonnet, Alain
  Artificial intelligence.
  Translation of: L'intelligence artificielle.
  Includes bibliographies and index.
  1. Artificial intelligence.   I. Title.
Q335.B6613   1985   006.3   85-16772
ISBN 0-13-048869-0 (pbk.)

British Library Cataloguing in Publication Data

Bonnet, Alain
  Artificial intelligence: promise and performance.
  1. Artificial intelligence – Juvenile literature
  I. Title   II. L'intelligence artificielle. English
  001.53'5   Q335.4

ISBN 0-13-048869-0

ISBN 0-13-048869-0

PRENTICE-HALL, INC., *Englewood Cliffs New Jersey*
PRENTICE-HALL INTERNATIONAL, UK., LTD., *London*
PRENTICE-HALL OF AUSTRALIA PTY., LTD., *Sydney*
PRENTICE-HALL CANADA, INC., *Toronto*
PRENTICE-HALL OF INDIA PRIVATE LIMITED, *New Delhi*
PRENTICE-HALL OF JAPAN, INC., *Tokyo*
PRENTICE-HALL OF SOUTHEAST ASIA PTE., LTD., *Singapore*
EDITORA PRENTICE-HALL DO BRASIL LTDA., *Rio de Janeiro*
PRENTICE-HALL HISPANOAMERICANA, S.A., *Mexico*
WHITEHALL BOOKS LIMITED, *Wellington, New Zealand*

Printed in Great Britain by A. Wheaton & Co., Ltd., Exeter

1 2 3 4 5 89 88 87 86 85

Contents

PART FIVE: PERSPECTIVES FOR THE FUTURE 187

Acknowledgements

I offer my warmest and most sincere thanks to the following:

- my colleagues (who even so are my friends) who have had the patience, the courage and the self-denial to read the earlier drafts of this book and whose comments, given so freely and without restraint, have resulted in considerable, sometimes spectacular, improvements. Among these are Daniel Kayser, Jean-Paul Haton, Jean-Michel Truong Ngoc, Jacques Harry and Pierre Zweigenbaum.

- Jacques Pitrat, pioneer of Artificial Intelligence in France, who has been good enough to write the Preface that follows.

- all those students, teachers and research workers at the Ecole Nationale Supérieure des Télécommunications who have put such excellent questions to me and to which I am now replying, although I could not do so at the time.

- Irma Gomez and Jacqueline Collene for their excellent typing.

- Gerard Sandier for his entertaining illustrations.

- the authorities at Télécommunications who have allowed me the materials and the time needed to produce this book.

A.B.

Preface

When Alain Bonnet asked me, in a friendly way, if I would write a preface to this book I began to ask myself just what is a preface? What seemed to me to be the best definition was also rather demoralizing: that part of the book that no-one reads. I then turned my thoughts to the different kinds of preface there might be.

First, it seemed, there is the Preface Eulogistic. Its aim is to point out the merits of the book and of the author, and is essential when these are not very evident: the message then is, "don't judge the author by this book, he has many other good qualities". The need does not arise here for the book is excellent.

Second is the Preface Reflexive. Here the purpose is to eulogize not the author but the writer of the preface and the theme is: "of course, this book isn't at all bad but if you want to read something really good on the subject you should read what I've written". This reminds me of a certain General, a master of this style, who in recommending his aide-de-camp for a decoration wrote: "Never hesitated to follow his chief in the most dangerous situations".

After so incautious a revelation I cannot continue along this track, so I must turn to the third type, the Preface Explanatory. This is essential when the book is incomprehensible. I recall a novel by Faulkner where I had confidently skipped the preface only to find myself plunged without warning into a recital of events by, apparently, a mental defective. Tail between my legs, I went into reverse to find out who was speaking and what was happening. Here again such a preface is unnecessary, the book being perfectly clear.

Fourthly is the Preface Perfidious. This showers praises on the author who has been so rash as to ask his dear friend and colleague to write a preface to his book; after having seen the author congratulated for the austerity of his style and for having overcome every temptation to make any concession to the tastes of the public he is addressing, the reader is in no doubt about what he has to face.

Fortunately for me there is a fifth type, the Preface Quixotic. When someone gives us the opportunity to talk about ourselves we seize it and get up on our favourite hobby-horse and this is what I propose to do.

The subject of artificial intelligence has often been criticized for not concerning itself with immediate applications. It is true that we are often working towards a goal that is very ambitious but of a long-term nature; but there are two fields in which genuine applications have already been made: understanding questions phrased in natural language and construction of expert systems. One of the merits of this book is its emphasis on these two aspects. Alain Bonnet has described both in considerable detail and he is extremely well qualified to do so because he has made original contributions in both areas.

There is, however, an indirect application of artificial intelligence techniques that could have immediate fall-out effects. Humans can use the knowledge that has been gathered together to form an expert system. What is of prime importance is that as soon as a body of expertise has been put down in black and white, it can be easily transmitted to another expert or even to a newcomer to the field; not even an expert knows everything and everyone can benefit from the experience of one's colleagues. If an expert leaves his/her company, that can be a catastrophic loss for the company, possibly even for mankind if he/she is going into retirement. In this case a body of knowledge may be lost for ever. None of this need happen if the knowledge has been put into an expert system for then even someone who knows nothing of the subject can quickly build up to a new level of competence.

Yet another beneficial consequence is that, when an expert system has been constructed, anyone can see just what constitutes the expertise. Many individuals fail to become expert in some field, simply because they do not know what is required and are unwilling to risk aiming at a goal of which they have only a vague idea. Take mathematics as an example. One of the aims of teaching this subject is to create good mathematical specialists, but we have to admit that the process has not proved very satisfactory, because few pupils achieve any significant level of expertise. Everyone would agree that part of the required expertise is a knowledge of certain theorems, but that is not enough: there is also a need for a stock of reasoning processes that will indicate which method to use when attacking a problem, given that it has certain characteristics. The textbooks give too few examples of knowledge of this type, and without knowing the rules it is usually impossible to solve the problem. To the pupil the mathematician is a magician with a special gift, the mathematical genius. These rules can be put into an expert system and all can see and study them; pupils can use them, but more importantly they can discover their importance and find what ideas they contain, and this will give them the idea of looking for analogies when faced with an unfamiliar situation rather than waiting passively for inspiration to dawn. This principle is valid in every field. If I am to edit a text in a foreign language I need to have more expertise in that language than is represented by the words in any of the present types of dictionary. I should like the dictionary to tell me exactly which words can be used to represent a certain concept, and to what extent the different qualities that characterize the concept are conveyed by the various possible words. I have learned a great deal about the English language as a result of studying the knowledge incorporated into programs for understanding this language, such as those of Winograd and of Schank. But I should very much have liked to find somewhere the expertise that would tell me how to write a preface.

Jacques Pitrat

Part One

Introduction

1

Aims and Basic Concepts of Artificial Intelligence

Artificial Intelligence (AI) is the discipline that aims to understand the nature of human intelligence through the construction of computer programs that imitate intelligent behavior.

To say that a program solves a problem, or takes a decision on the basis of a description of some situation, means that the program itself finds the method to be used in order to solve the problem or to reach the decision, calling on a wide range of reasoning processes that have been incorporated into it. This is an important development beyond what is conventionally understood of information technology, where the reasoning is done by a human being and the machine used primarily because of its speed of calculation.

Whilst we cannot define human intelligence in general we can highlight a number of criteria by which it can be judged, such as the ability to make abstractions or generalizations, to draw analogies between different situations and to adapt to new ones, to detect and correct mistakes in order to improve future performance, and so on. AI is often, and erroneously, equated with cybernetics: this latter subject is concerned with the mathematical properties of feed-back systems and treats the human being as an automaton, whereas the former is concerned with the cognitive processes brought into play by the human being in order to perform what we regard as intelligent tasks. Such tasks can be of very varied nature, for example the understanding of some account spoken or written in a natural language, playing chess or bridge, solving a puzzle or a mathematical problem, writing a poem, making a medical diagnosis, finding one's way from Brooklyn to Philadelphia. The AI researcher goes about his work by first selecting an activity that is generally acknowledged to be "intelligent", framing some hypotheses concerning the information and the reasoning processes used in the course of this activity, incorporating these into a computer program and then observing the behavior of the program. A study of the limitations of the program suggests modifications to the theoretical basis and thus to the program itself, giving a changed behavior suggesting further modifications, and so on.

The problems with which AI deals are dominated by the combinatorial explosion: that is, the number of possibilities is so great that an optimal solution (assuming that one exists) cannot be found by a straightforward search through these, either because the time needed would be much too long or the process would need much too much memory capacity, whether human or computer. Thus the number of possible positions in a game of chess has been estimated[1] as about 10^{120}; it is clearly impossible to examine the full set or to store all these together with a measure of the value of each position. There is in fact a fundamental difference in attitude between the mathematician and the AI worker in this context. The methematician seeks to prove that a solution to a problem exists (he may, of course, show that no solution exists) and is not concerned with the means by which the solution might be obtained; the AI worker, in contrast, is looking for a solution which may not be strictly correct or optimal but which is acceptable to whoever is concerned with the problem and which can be found within an acceptable time and in real-life conditions in which some of the required data may not be obtainable. Consider, for example, the game of "Mastermind". The mathematician will aim to prove that there is an algorithm that will give the solution in, say, at most 7 moves, whilst the AI worker will use all his skills to construct a program that uses sound processes of reasoning and is not primarily interested in knowing whether or not there may be an unfavorable case in which the solution is not reached before the eighth move. The predominant attitude in AI is that good principles of organization are more important than speed of calculation; mathematics enters more at the logical level, and whilst the best understood logical system is that of deductive logic this is certainly less important than inductive or inferential logic for most of our intelligent activities. The term "inference" will be used throughout this book to convey the ideas of both induction and deduction. In addition to this use at the logical level, mathematics—at a fairly elementary level—is employed in obtaining estimates of the amount of memory and of processing time needed for the solution of a problem.

The rest of this introductory section attempts to formulate a characterization of an AI computer program. The criteria put forward relate on the one hand to the types of problem that are attacked—their solution requires a certain amount of intelligence, and a general solution is not known—and on the other to the methods employed, taking advantage of whatever is known about human intelligence.

Symbolic representation

The first characteristic of AI programs is that they deal mainly with non-numerical symbols and thus contrast strongly with the commonly accepted view that the computer can deal only with figures. At the lowest level the machine is composed of binary devices which exist in either of two states conventionally named 0 and 1; but this is only for convenience, and the states could equally well have been called Blue and Red: the "0, 1" convention has contributed strongly to the spread of the view that the computer can understand only "yes" and "no", and has no power of understanding nuances of meaning between these. But at the equivalent level, that of the neurons, human understanding rests equally on binary states; showing that with sufficiently complex combinations of such states high-level concepts can be represented and elaborate decision processes constructed. The possibility of expressing these high-level concepts in terms of the symbols manipulated by the computer enables the decision processes to be simulated.

Of course, there is no reason why an AI program should not perform numerical calculations where necessary; but the results will generally be used at a conceptually higher level, that is, their significance or symbolic value will generally enter into the reasoning process performed by the program. For example, a medical diagnosis program will use the information "patient's temperature is 100°F" in the symbolic form "patient has low fever", even though the original information was numerical.

An example of purely symbolic information is provided by plant pathology, where the statement "mildew is a fungus" could be used in a reasoning process in the form "damage caused by fungi in general can be caused by mildew in particular". This type of reasoning or inference is usually called *inheritance* or *transmission* of properties, and is of fundamental importance in AI.

Heuristics

The second characteristic of AI programs is that they attack problems for which no general algorithm is known—that is, there is no known sequence of steps guaranteed to lead to the solution. Given that no algorithm is known, recourse is had to "heuristics",[2] that is, to informal (in contrast to formal) methods which are not guaranteed to succeed. The heuristic procedure consists in choosing a method of attack which seems promising, while keeping open the possibility of changing to another if the first seems not to be leading quickly to a solution.

A program for solving quadratic equations would not be counted as an AI program, because an algorithm for the general solution is known. In contrast, a program for symbolic integration could rank as an AI program, for such a program would try one change of variable (i.e. one method) in order to simplify the function to be integrated, and then another if the first did not succeed and so on.

Chess-playing programs are a fertile field for AI, because no method is known by which the best move in any given position can be determined. This is so because, on the one hand, there are too many possibilities for an exhaustive search to be made, and on the other because little or nothing is known of the reasoning on which the best players base their moves—either because they themselves are not consciously aware of this or because they do not wish to reveal their reasons. Some of the detractors of AI, for example Herbert Dreyfus,[3] used to predict that no computer program would ever reach the level of a good human player; but this has long been disproved, and today (1985) the best programs can beat all but a few hundreds of human players.

Knowledge representation

AI programs, in contrast to statistical programs, contain a representation of knowledge, that is, a correspondence between the external world and a symbolic reasoning system. This knowledge can usually be studied and understood in what we may call human terms, because the symbols used for its representation are seldom numerical. For example, a medical diagnosis program (see Chapter 16) may use the following rule to suggest that a sick patient has influenza.

"If the patient has a high temperature, muscular pains and a headache, there is a strong possibility of influenza."

Such a rule would be given explicitly in the program's knowledge base and not hidden somewhere in pages of low-level language.* A statistical program will have extensive tables of correlations between symptoms and possible illnesses, from which it would be very difficult to justify the solution provided by the AI program.

Further, a well thought-out program for medical diagnosis will include features such as "weak legs" and "stiff legs" as being two abnormal states of "patient's legs"; these "legs" being linked to other parts of the patient's body. Existing statistical programs do not include this type of "commonsense" knowledge.

---

* There is no pejorative force in this term. It is usual to distinguish between high-level languages, meaning languages close to the human user, and low-level, close to the machine.

It is the separation, as clearly as possible, of the knowledge base from the mechanisms that use this knowledge that is very characteristic of the methodology of AI programs. The knowledge items are expressed as clearly as possible, so that their meaning is easily understood. All that is written in a programming language, and is therefore difficult for anyone but an information science expert to understand, is the set of mechanisms that interpret these items, such as whatever decides that such and such an inferential rule should be called into play by such and such a statement. We shall return to this point in the chapter on expert systems.

Syntactic analysis of a language is another example of this methodological separation, here between the rules that govern the legality of declarative phrases (that is, their grammar) and the interpreter of this grammar that decides whether or not a given phrase can be generated by the production rules. In the first natural-language analyzers[4] the grammatical rules were integrated into the mechanisms for using these, with the result that it proved very difficult to increase the area of the language to which the grammar applied because some part of the program had to be changed whenever a new grammatical rule was added.

Incomplete data

A fourth fundamental characteristic of an AI program is the capacity to provide some solution even if not all the data relevant to the problem is available at the time when the solution is required. It often happens in medicine, for example, that the results of certain laboratory tests are not available when a decision which would make use of these has to be taken, and cannot wait.

The consequence of the data being incomplete is simply that the conclusions are less certain, or less "good" in some sense—with the possibility of being wrong in some cases. In the real world a decision often has to be made in the absence of all the relevant data, with the consequences that the wrong conclusions will sometimes be drawn. It can happen also that the absence of complete data is inherent in the problem; an example is a game of bridge, where each player knows the contents of only two hands and must make error-prone estimates of the distribution of the unknown cards, using the bidding as a guide.

Conflicting data

A fifth characteristic is the ability to take account of data items that are more or less in contradiction with one another; these are what I call conflicting data, or more simply data corrupted by errors. Consider the following example, where A, B, C represent observable events and the numbers the strengths of the various statements on a scale ranging from − 10, meaning that the statement is certainly false, to + 10, certainly true. In both cases it is given that both A and B have been observed.

1. If A then C (+ 5)
   If B then C (− 3)
2. If A then C (+ 10)
   If B then C (− 10)

In Case 1 there is conflict but not contradiction. The laws are inductive: it can often happen that an event, say C, is likely to be observed after another, say A, has been observed; and is unlikely to be observed after a third, say B, has been observed. Two opposing beliefs have to be combined, and the situation is that the simultaneous occurrence of A and B is infrequent.

In Case 2 however there is a flat contradiction, for which there are two possible explanations. The first is that at least one of the laws is wrong, and that, for example, account has not been taken of some further condition that would restrict the field of application of the law. The second, which is of more interest, is that an error of observation has been made and that one or other of the events A or B did not in fact occur. In an actual case we should resolve the contradiction by keeping whichever of the two laws was the more consistent with the rest of our knowledge.

Ability to learn

Another criterion for intelligent behavior is the ability to learn from mistakes, that is, to improve performance by taking account of past errors: but it must be said that few human beings would count as intelligent if this were applied with 100% rigor. This faculty is related to the capacity for generalizing, for drawing analogies and for selectively discarding information. AI researchers have not yet been very successful in their work on the first two of these. It has proved difficult to specify the region within which a generalization is valid, which is equivalent to saying that it is difficult to avoid making false generalizations; and it is equally difficult to decide the context within which an analogy is valid. The third factor, that of selective discarding, represents a very subtle problem. The computer is often valued for its property, unlike the human mind, of forgetting nothing; but it is precisely the ability to forget that gives man his ability to learn, by putting aside unimportant details and replacing individual facts by procedures—clearly intelligent—that enable him to recover these facts when he needs them. Thus the problem of giving the computer a learning ability similar to that of the human being is that of simulating in the machine the processes by means of which man distinguishes between facts that are important, and are therefore to be remembered, and those that are not important and can therefore be forgotten. What can from one point of view be considered a weakness of the human mind is in fact the source of its immense capacity for learning: the ability to extract the essence of a set of facts, rather than to store them all systematically, is one of the great human strengths. Intelligence is quite the opposite of the ability to play the "20 Questions" game well, for this is one of the easiest skills to develop in a computer: erudition is not intelligence.

This explains, to my mind, the relative lack of interest in database work shown so far by AI researchers. However, information scientists who are concerned with databases are now beginning to be conscious of the limitations of present methods of approach, and are increasingly seeking to build reasoning abilities into their systems. It is likely that an AI researcher tackling this problem from scratch would organize the storage differently, in a way that was more conducive to associations of ideas and to searches by analogies.

Mimic human behavior at all costs?

The last point that I shall touch on in this introductory chapter is the one that gives rise to most controversy among AI workers: should a program attack a problem in the same way as a human solver would, or is this a question of little importance, provided that it reaches a solution by some means or other? I feel that the position that any individual takes on this question depends upon his response to another question: in developing what we have called artificial intelligence, are we aiming to understand the working of human intelligence or are we simply regarding the machine as a means for processing information for utilitarian purposes? Clearly, anyone who takes the first line on the first question will also take the first line on the second, and similarly for the second lines. The type of research which any individual takes up will of course be strongly influenced by his attitude on these questions; this does not mean that it is necessary to mimic a process in order to understand it, but doing so will certainly increase the ability to examine the details of its mechanisms.

It should not be inferred from the distinction just made that programs written with the aim of imitating human reasoning are necessarily not "useful" in the utilitarian sense: usefulness at all costs is not the aim of research and should not dictate the methods to be used. Care should be taken to ensure that these methods are based on sound concepts before any questions of performance are considered.

The position taken in this book is clearly that corresponding to the first choice in answer to the questions, that of seeking to understand human intelligence. This raises the further question, how can we hope to imitate human behavior when we do not understand its method of working, and moreover when we know that different human beings behave in different ways? We can however be certain about ways in which humans do *not* behave in various circumstances, and this enables us to eliminate many possibilities. Consider for example the process of understanding language. It is clear that we do not usually read a phrase several times in order to understand it, so that any computer program based on such a process could be described as "psychologically invalid". It is also clear that we do not start by constructing a syntactic tree for a phrase and then proceed to derive a semantic interpretation of this: all evidence shows that the two processes are closely interwoven. A program using such a separation does little to explain our own methods, but this approach has been used because it is easier to implement than integrating the two.

In the other direction, introspection and the results of psycho-linguistic experiments with human subjects can provide invaluable information on what can be retained most easily in the mind, what inferences can be drawn from material read or heard, and what predictions made by the reader or listener are later verified or shown to be wrong. There can be close links between the results of such experiments and the way in which programs imitating these processes are used.

Finally, the capacity of a program to improve its performance by learning is a good indicator of the relevance of the structures it uses in simulating human reasoning; if these do not admit of any learning—possibly because of the inherent properties of the sub-structures on which they are based—they are not true analogs of those that we ourselves use. As is traditional in science, we accept that a theory is valid only to the extent that it is not called into question by observation.

AI influences many disciplines, especially computer science because programs have to be written to test its theories; and since these programs are of necessity interactive, it has contributed to the development of interactive languages. Further, the need for programs that can evolve as ideas change and develop has had an important influence on program methodology generally. The lessons learned from logic have led to a formalization of the reasoning process which, whilst often over-simplifying, has provided a starting point for the representation of this process. Links with linguistics are necessary for the understanding of natural languages, even though linguists and AI researchers often take different points of view; and there are links also with psychology, the neuro-sciences, biology and philosophy, although probably fewer than there should be. These interactions with other subjects are analyzed very well by Margaret Boden[5] in her introductory book on artificial intelligence.

Topics treated in this book

Three areas of AI are of prime importance at this time: interpreting images, understanding natural languages and expert systems, and techniques for learning. Image interpretation is a subject in its own right with its own techniques; it requires a book for itself alone, a task beyond the competence of the present author: the reader who is interested should consult Brady[6] or Pratt.[7]

The first third of this book deals with the understanding of natural languages and the second with the need to make inferences in order to understand items of knowledge and thus to have suitable means for representing these. Most of the remaining third is concerned with expert systems, a subject which is rich in applications and which is revolutionizing information technology. Their use in computer assisted teaching is studied here, also the learning methods by means of which a program can use experience to improve its performance, and several examples are described. The book concludes with a consideration of what may be expected of AI in the future.

Notes and references

[1] An average chess game is of 80 individual moves, that is, 40 by each player, with about 30 possible legal moves at each position; thus the number of possible positions on the board is of the order of $30^{80} \approx (2^5)^{80} = (2^{10})^{40} \approx (10^3)^{40} = 10^{120}$.

[2] Polya, G. (1945), *How to solve it, a new aspect of mathematical method.* Princeton, Princeton University Press.
George Polya is one of the greatest mathematical teachers. He has strongly criticized mathematicians who make a habit of giving the solution in a way that shows nothing of how that solution was found. He, in contrast, believes it to be of fundamental importance to teach the heuristic methods that are actually used in seeking solutions: for example, breaking down a problem into simpler sub-problems, trying to reduce a problem to one that one already knows how to solve, making a drawing, and so on.

[3] Dreyfus, H. L. (1972), *What computers can't do: a critique of artificial reason.* New York, Harper & Row.

[4] Winograd, T. (1972), *Understanding natural language.* Edinburgh, Edinburgh University Press.

[5] Boden, M. (1977), *Artificial intelligence and natural man.* New York, Basic Books.

[6] Brady, M. (1983), "Computational approach to image understanding", *ACM computing surveys,* Vol. 14, pp. 3-71.

[7] Pratt, W. (1978), *Digital image processing.* New York, Wiley.

Part Two

Understanding Natural Languages

2
Some Criteria

Introduction

The aim of this chapter is to point out the different lines of activity that can be distinguished under the general name of "understanding natural languages".

The first is what I shall call the utilitarian activity and is what is often referred to as man-machine interaction (MMI). This does not attack any problems of understanding human behavior, but only those of communication between human beings and the computer. We want to make it possible for this communication to take place in a language that is as close as possible to a natural language, meaning by this term a language that is associated with a human culture such as English, French, Spanish, Arabic, etc. What is needed is a bridge between such a language and the "artificial" low-level language appropriate to the machine. A first step in this direction was the development of what are called high-level programming languages, such as Fortran, Algol, LISP, which are translated into machine language by programs called compilers. Such languages are easier to learn and to use than the machine languages, but are still artificial. Our problem is that we wish to conduct a dialog with the machine in a natural manner, without having to learn a programming language, and we therefore need to find a way to translate the human user's requirements, supplied to the machine by means of an input terminal, into a form that the machine can understand and act on. For example, there is often a need to query a database by putting questions of the form, "Which employees of John Smith & Co. are paid more than £10,000 per annum?" This would be translated into something like

(?X (NAME-EMPLOYER ?X = JOHN SMITH & CO)
(SALARY ?X > 10,000))

which would indicate that we want the names of all those individuals x who are such that Employer-of-x = John Smith & Co and Salary-of-x > 10,000. This form, which is internal to the machine, can be regarded as the statement of a procedure that can be carried out in a programming language, and is typical of the queries made of databases in order to extract information. The transformation of the natural-language form of the request into a form that has some significance for the database assumes that "John Smith & Co." is to be interpreted as the name of a company, that this company has employees and that we are interested in their salaries (not in their home addresses or number of children) and, more precisely, in those whose salaries exceed a stated amount. The use of such techniques can have striking results, because they enable a dialog to be conducted in a natural way which can give the illusion of considerable mutual understanding between man and machine; important developments can certainly be expected of this line of activity in the coming years.

The second line of activity is what I shall call the linguistic or logical line. The central question here is to decide if any given phrase could actually be said in ordinary life. The current practice among language scholars is to mark with an asterisk any phrases that seem strange to them and then to ask what it is that makes them strange; we may call this the legalistic aspect. Another characteristic here is the regarding of a language as an independent object without any consideration of its cognitive or communicative functions; the best known proponent of this view is Noam Chomsky,[1] who introduced the distinction between competence and performance—that is, between what one theoretically can say or understand and what one actually can do—and for whom a language is an object of which the formal or mathematical properties are to be studied, without reference to the way in which it is used. Terry Winograd[2] has compared this attitude to that of physicists who study mechanics without taking friction into account. Chomsky is interested in formal grammars, that is, in systems of formal rules governing the possible arrangements of the basic symbols. He has aimed to define the properties of "universal grammars", idealized objects which he defines as "a system of principles, conditions and rules which form the elements or properties of every human language".[3] Chomsky has recognized[4] that the grammars in which he is interested are much too complex to be learned by humans, starting as they do from general principles—the universal grammars—which he considers innate, that is, genetically coded. Thus these are unlikely to be of the same type as the grammars we use in analyzing phrases.

The third line of activity is the one I shall attempt to support in this book. It rejects the simplifying assumption of a fixed and unambiguous relation between the superficial form of a phrase—meaning the linear sequence of characters organized into words, with the words organized into phrases—and the deep structure that carries its meaning. Instead, the view is taken that inferential processes are brought into play as soon as we start to read any phrase or text and that the understanding of a text is not essentially different from the understanding of anything else. In every case the information we receive is influenced by everything that we know already. Syntax certainly plays a role, but not a fundamental one, and we certainly do not separate our analysis into two phases, the first constructing a syntactic tree and the second making a semantic analysis of this. This line of attack is the only one that attempts to explain how our minds work, and over the past 15 years or so its most enthusiastic proponent has been Roger Schank.[5] The aim here is not to produce programs which, as it were, understand natural language at whatever cost, but to display and explain our methods of understanding. In this work theories of understanding are formulated and then tested by means of programs that have been developed so as, it is hoped, to operate analogously to our own processes, taking into account our subjective reactions, knowledge and motivations.

The section of the book devoted to natural language is divided into seven chapters. The present chapter, Chapter 2, gives some basic criteria by which "understanding" of such languages may be judged. Chapter 3 describes the first, unfruitful, attempts at automatic translation and the first techniques used in conducting as natural as possible a conversation with a computer. Chapter 4 describes the first programs written to analyze individual phrases, using, in most cases, formal grammars; the main problems that arise are described here. Chapter 5 gives some of the techniques used in this analysis, that is, the methods for converting the natural form of a phrase into its internal representation in the machine. Chapter 6 describes some specific aspects of spoken text, as distinct from written. Chapter 7 introduces the practical problem of natural-language interfaces between the user and the machine. Finally, Chapter 8 describes a change in the direction of development of ideas that is of fundamental importance: the center of interest is no longer the transformation of a phrase from the form in which it is input to the computer to an internal form that should carry its meaning, but rather the understanding of the plot of a story and the motivations of the people involved. The formal analysis of a phrase is less and less separated from its context and from the inferences that can be drawn at the time of reading, whether this reading is by a computer or by a human being.

Some criteria for "understanding"

Just as I do not feel capable of giving a definition of intelligence— although I could give various criteria, each relating to a different aspect such as the ability to generalize or to learn from experience and so improve future performance—I shall not attempt to define the concept of understanding, whether by man or machine. Nevertheless, a number of criteria can be put forward, each reflecting one of several degrees of understanding.

1. The capacity to respond to questions in an appropriate manner. The strength of this criterion resides of course in the requirement of "appropriateness"; and whilst this cannot be defined in absolute terms, various degrees can be identified. Thus if the question were, "Is Rome the capital of France?" the simple reply "No" would be appropriate but, "No, that is Paris" or, "No, Rome is the capital of Italy" would be more so.

2. The capacity to paraphrase a statement, explaining its meaning in other terms.

3. The capacity to make inferences, that is, to give possible or probable consequences of what has just been said. This criterion includes the others.

4. The capacity to translate from one language to another. The three criteria outlined above assume a certain capacity for abstraction, reflecting the possibility of forming a semantic or conceptual representation of the various causal or dependent relations among the constituents of a phrase, while taking as little account as possible of the superficial structure. It will be shown later, in the discussion of the failure of the early attempts at automatic translation, that the reasons for these failures are to be found precisely in the absence of any capacity for abstraction. We should note that making inferences can include both making explicit what is only implicit in the given text and divining the motivations of the people for the actions that are described.

5. The capacity to identify references. An important constituent of our ability to understand is an awareness that the same object or person can be referred to in different ways, such as when the name of a person or group is replaced by a personal pronoun. Finding the correct referent can sometimes demand great knowledge or reasoning power.

6. The successful passing of the Turing test for intelligence. The English mathematician Alan Turing imagined the following test. Suppose we are using a terminal—a keyboard and visual display screen today, a teletype in Turing's time—which we know communicates sometimes with a computer program and sometimes with another person, but we never know with which. If after a certain time we cannot decide which responses have been made by the program, then we must say that the program is intelligent. The reader who is interested in this idea should read Douglas Hofstadter's book.[6] It is hardly necessary to say that no program so far has succeeded in passing this test; most of the few that have sustained the illusion for a few minutes simulate the behavior of psychiatric cases.

The first five criteria relate to different aspects of the process of understanding, whilst the sixth involves all of these; each of the five would have to be satisfied before the test of the sixth could be passed.

Notes and references

[1] Chomsky, N. (1965), *Aspects of the theory of syntax*. Cambridge, Mass., MIT Press.
[2] Winograd, T. (1977), "On some contested suppositions of generative linguistics about the scientific study of language". Stanford Artificial Intelligence Laboratory, *Memorandum, AIM-300*.
This appeared in the review *Cognition* (1976). It is a brilliant response to an article by Dresher and Hornstein[7] who maintained that AI research had contributed nothing to the theory of language development.
[3] Chomsky, N. (1975), *Reflections on language*. New York, Pantheon Books.
[4] Chomsky, N. (1982), "Rules and representation" in *The behavioral and brain sciences*.
[5] Schank, R. C. (1975), *Conceptual information processing*. New York, North Holland.
[6] Hofstadter, D. (1977), *Godel, Escher, Bach. An eternal golden braid*. New York, Basic Books.
A brilliant work in which the author examines the points common to the drawings of Escher, the canons of Bach, and Godel's Theorem. He gives interesting reflections on the phenomenon of self-reference (e.g., "This phrase no verb") and on recursivity, the latter being of fundamental importance in information science and in AI.
[7] Dresher, B. E., Hornstein, N. (1976), "On some supposed contributions of artificial intelligence to the scientific study of language". *Cognition* 4, pp. 321-398.

3
The Era of Natural Language Processing

Introduction

The term "processing", rather than "understanding", is used deliberately because the period dealt with in this chapter is characterized by the absence of any internal representation of concepts detected in the text; there is simply formal manipulation of the symbols, in the sense just described. We can also include statistical analyses of text under the same term, such as counting the numbers of times various words are used in a political speech. These manipulative and statistical methods do not form part of the subject of AI but were the precursors to its methods, and for this reason are described briefly in this chapter.

First attempts at automatic translation

We can locate the first ideas for translation from one language to another by computer program towards the end of 1946, in a discussion between Warren Weaver and Andrew Booth;[1] their view at the time was that the methods used to decipher secret codes, which were based on the use of tables of relative frequencies of letters and words, could be applied to translation. Thus they did not aim to achieve any understanding of the messages conveyed by the texts but thought only in terms of formal processing of sequences of letters. The difficulties they foresaw were those of incorporating sufficiently complete dictionaries of the two languages and of dealing with the multiple meanings that most words have and with the different word orders used by different languages, even when they are structurally similar.

AI-C

The first translation programs to be written incorporated dictionaries in which the full conjugation of every verb was given explicitly rather than the infinitive together with processes for finding the different endings. The first program to translate from Russian to English produced as output a series of lists giving for each Russian word all the possible translations into English, with no decision as to which was correct: thus not even the stage of word-for-word translation had been reached.

Interest in machine translation declined rapidly during the 1960s after about fifteen years of unfruitful effort. In his lectures Bar Hillel showed that a knowledge base of encyclopedic size would have to be held in the machine, which he clearly regarded as unrealistic. To understand why the work of these years produced so little result we must remember that no-one at that time had any idea of how to instruct a computer in grammar, that programs were still being written in machine language, and that the idea of a recursive language[2] had made little headway.

The lesson learned from these efforts was that translation without understanding was impossible. Means had to be found to represent the meaning of a phrase or a piece of text, and to resolve the ambiguities that could be presented by certain words, which would necessitate an appeal to the context or perhaps to a model of the world relevant to the text. Research in the field of machine translation was taken up again after an interval of ten or more years, when there was a better understanding of these needs.

The pre-semantic period

Two approaches characterize the period 1960 to 1970, having in common the feature of not looking for any meaning in a phrase, that is, not attempting to set up any symbolic representation of its relation to the real world. The first method consists of using the rules of a transformation grammar to produce, by successive transformation, a sequence of phrases until one that matches the given phrase is found;[3] but such a method is made useless by the combinatorial explosion, a consequence of the enormous number of transformations that can be derived from an initial structure. The second approach used keywords or word sequences, called patterns, to extract information from the phrase to be analyzed.[4] A typical program using this approach was ELIZA. This is now of only historical interest but shows very well how such programs can give an illusion of understanding.

ELIZA simulates a psychiatrist of the "free association" school with whom a patient can conduct a conversation in natural language. In the following example the patient speaks first and ELIZA's responses are given in capitals:

Men are all alike
IN WHAT WAY?
They're always bugging us in some way or other
CAN YOU THINK OF A SPECIFIC EXAMPLE?
Well, my boyfriend made me come here
YOUR BOYFRIEND MADE YOU COME HERE?
He says I'm depressed much of the time
I AM SORRY TO HEAR YOU ARE DEPRESSED

The program works on a very simple principle. It has a store of pairs of words or groups of words, the first of each pair being a pattern found in the phrase and the second the program's response; thus the same response is generated whenever the same pattern is recognized. An example is

(* mother *) → (TELL ME ABOUT YOUR PARENTS)

where the asterisks can be substituted for any word or phrase (so that what precedes or follows "mother" is irrelevant) and → states that this is the program's response. This would give this dialog:

My mother used to beat me when I was little
TELL ME ABOUT YOUR PARENTS

which seems natural enough, but it would also produce:

Prince Charles's mother is going to France tomorrow
TELL ME ABOUT YOUR PARENTS

which is much less so.

In its most highly developed version, ELIZA could make various transformations of the parts of the pattern represented by the asterisks. In particular it could replace the first person singular by the second, and so produce an appropriate and grammatically correct phrase; this is shown in the response ". . . YOU ARE DEPRESSED . . ." to the pattern ". . . I am depressed . . ." in the above example.

The limitations of such an approach are clear. For one thing, it is unrealistic to expect to foresee, and provide responses to, all possible phrases; and for another, nothing representing the meaning of the phrases or concepts that are manipulated is built into the program. Thus such a program has no bearing on the processes involved in the understanding of a language.

A few other programs of this period are still well known because they took the first tentative steps towards showing some degree of understanding. One of these, STUDENT,[5] conceived by Daniel Bobrow of MIT, solved simple algebraic problems expressed in a natural language. It also made use of patterns, such as

(*1 is *2 times *3)
(what is the *1 of *2?)

STUDENT's method of solution was generally based on the rules of simple proportion and the response consisted of "filling in the blanks" in fixed patterns. William Colby's program PARRY[6] which simulates the behavior of a paranoiac can, like ELIZA, conduct a dialog in a natural language. Its method of working is more complex because parameters associated with certain words such as FEAR, SHAME, ANGER give different intensities to these according to the phrases input by the "patient" and thus cause the response to vary as the context of the conversation varies. However, the criticisms made of ELIZA apply equally to STUDENT and to PARRY.

Notes and references

[1] Weaver, W. (1955), "Translation", in Locke & Booth (eds.) *Machine translation of languages*, New York, Technology Press of MIT and Wiley.

[2] A program is said to be recursive if it can call itself. Not all programming languages allow this: COBOL for example does not.

[3] Petrick, S. R. (1973), "Transformational analysis" in Rustin (ed.) *Natural language processing*, New York, Algorithmics Press, pp. 27-41.

[4] Weizenbaum, J. (1966), "Eliza, a computer program for the study of natural language communication between man and machine". *CACM* 9, pp. 36-45. Weizenbaum has since written a very moralistically-oriented book [*Computer power and human reason* (1976), San Francisco, Freeman] in which, in common with some biologists commenting on the Asilomar conference on genetic engineering, he warns of the danger of simulating on the computer certain intellectual processes that should remain typical of humans.

[5] Bobrow, D. G. (1968), "Natural language input for a computer problem-solving system", in Minsky, M. (ed.), *Semantic information processing*, Cambridge, Mass., MIT Press, pp. 133-215 (the original article dated 1964).

[6] Colby, K. M., Weber, S., & Hilf, F. D. (1972), "Artificial paranoia" in *Artificial Intelligence* 3.

4
Understanding Isolated Phrases

This chapter describes the first programs that were able to analyze natural language with the aid of a grammar. The phrases were studied individually in isolation and the separate meanings obtained without any attempt at integration into a single piece of text. The first methods for representing meaning appeared in Roger Schank's theory of conceptual dependency.

The "semantic-syntactic" period

The start of this period, around 1970, reflected the abandoning of all hope of representing in the machine a grammar that would cover the whole of a language; the researchers limited themselves to restricted syntaxes closely linked to semantic tests. The first two programs marking this change were Winograd's SHRDLU[1] and Woods's LUNAR.[2] The period is characterized also by the aim of understanding only individual phrases without attempting to link these into a continuous text.

A complete program for understanding natural language is usually organized in the way shown in Fig. 4.1. Here the ovals contain the information to be processed, in its various forms, and the rectangles contain the sub-programs that perform the required transformations between these forms.

Since there is no general agreement on what an "internal representation" should contain, or on what the "meaning of a phrase" is, the separation into three sub-programs as shown here is quite arbitrary: the inferential process for example could start before the analysis ended. Further, not all programs contain inferential procedures; thus with a system for querying a database in a natural language the requirement is often simply to extract the correct item,

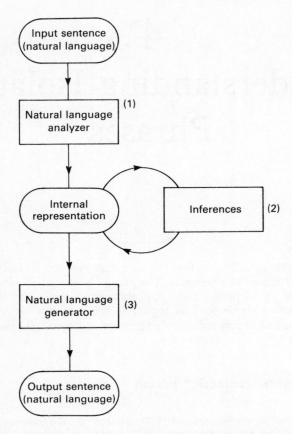

Figure 4.1   Standard schema for understanding natural language

although a more elaborate system may have means for interpreting an ambiguous request. Some workers, such as Coulon and Kayser,[3] prefer the concept of variable-depth interpretation to that of internal representation.

A text generator program is a very useful tool for showing what a system has understood; it puts the internal representation, which holds the meanings of the phrases, into a syntactically correct form.

Although we may cite T. Meehan[4] and D. McDonald,[5] research in this field has not attracted many AI workers, most of whom are interested in the phenomenon of understanding, so we shall only deal here with analysis and inference processes, and we shall not always treat these two mechanisms entirely separately.

The program that has remained the most famous in the history of artificial intelligence is undoubtedly SHRDLU,[1] produced at MIT by Terry

Winograd. This simulates a robot that can manipulate various objects such as cubes and pyramids laid out on a table and can converse in natural language with someone who gives it orders and asks questions about the objects. Winograd incorporated into his program a grammar derived from the "systemic grammars" of Halliday;[6] this is a system of logical networks expressing certain properties of syntactic units, in particular the mood, tense and voice (active or passive) of verbs. Items of semantic information are used during the analysis, thus reducing the number of structures that would be possible if syntactic criteria alone were applied.

The following is an example of an actual dialog with SHRDLU; its responses are in capitals:

How many things are on top of the green cubes?
I'M NOT SURE WHAT YOU MEAN BY "ON TOP OF" IN THE PHRASE "ON TOP OF THE GREEN CUBES". DO YOU MEAN
  1. DIRECTLY ON THE SURFACE
  2. ANYWHERE ON TOP?

2
THREE OF THEM
Had you touched any pyramid before you put the green one on the little cube?
YES, THE GREEN ONE
When did you pick it up?
WHILE I WAS STACKING UP THE RED CUBE, A LARGE RED BLOCK AND A LARGE GREEN CUBE
Why?
TO GET RID OF IT

  etc.

This shows that SHRDLU can solve problems requiring back-references to be worked out, such as deciding to which object a pronoun refers; also that it is "aware" of its own environment and is thus able to answer questions about the relations between different actions.

At about the same time William Woods applied his Augmented Transition Network (ATN—see next chapter) method to the development of a system for querying a database in natural language, which he called LUNAR. The database in question consisted of data on samples of lunar rocks collected by the NASA astronauts. The analysis of the questions took place in three stages:

(a) a syntactical analysis, producing the syntactic tree, or several if several were possible;

(b) a semantic analysis of the tree or trees, producing the internal form of the query;

(c) execution of this internal form, entailing a search of the database as requested in the natural-language form and output of the result in natural language.

A vocabulary of about 3,500 words is associated with the grammar; the analyzer can display a limited understanding of pronomial references and nested constructions such as relative clauses within a main clause.

LUNAR has had a very great influence on developments because of the technique (ATN) it uses in the analysis, which has become one of the most widely used during the past 10 years. Examples of the questions with which it can deal are:

— What is the average concentration of aluminium in highly alkaline rocks?
— How many samples contain P_2O_5?

MARGIE[7] is a program developed by C. Riesbeck, C. Rieger and N. Goldman under the direction of Roger Schank. It analyzes natural-language phrases which it transforms into "conceptual dependency" form. This process will be described later. The central part of the program can either paraphrase statements input into it, or can make inferences about the conceptual world it creates by speculating either on certain objects existing in this world or on the motivations of the people inhabiting it.

Here is an example of MARGIE's paraphrasing:

Input Statement: John strangled Mary
Output 1:   John killed Mary by strangling her
       2:        John suffocated Mary and she died because she could
                 not breathe
       3:        Mary died because she could not breathe and she could
                 not breathe because John wrung her neck

and here is an example of its inferential mode:

Input statement: John gave Mary an aspirin
Output 1:   John thought that Mary wanted an aspirin
       2:        Mary did not feel well
       3:        Mary wanted to get better

Another theory that has had great success among AI researchers, particularly those who do not regard syntax analysis as the universal solution to the problem of extraction of meaning is that of case-oriented grammars; a brief account is given below and the interested reader is referred to the original article by Charles Fillmore.[8]

The basic idea in such grammars is to consider the verb as the main constituent of a phrase and to study the relations of the various noun groups to this: in other words, to determine their grammatical case. In inflected languages the case of a noun is shown by a special termination, independently of the position in the sentence with respect to the verb; thus in Polish

Chłopiec je gruszkę   (the boy eats the pear)

could also be written

> Gruszke je chłopięc

because the fact that "the boy" (chłopiec) is the agent of the action is shown by the nominative ending "-ec", and that "the pear" (gruszkę) is the object is shown by the accusative ending "-ę". In English, nouns are never inflected for case; the closest equivalents are the forms He/Him, We/Us etc., for personal pronouns.

Fillmore points out that the traditional grammatical classifications such as subject, complement of object and so on serve only as superficial manifestations of deeper functions of case. His view is based on such observations as that in the three phrases

1. John broke the window with the hammer
2. The hammer broke the window
3. The window broke

the subject is different in each, although the action is the same; in other words, the three participants—John, the hammer and the window—can all fill the same lexical role, that of subject, although their functions are different. In contrast, the agent of the action (John), the instrument (the hammer) and the object (the window) remain the same in all three phrases although they are partially implicit in the last two.

Schank's theory of conceptual dependency is closely related to the idea of case-oriented grammars, the main difference being that he associates case with what are called *primitives* of verbs, defined in the next paragraph.

Theory of conceptual dependency

This was developed by Roger Schank[9] as a means of enabling simple phrases in natural language to be represented by schemas showing the semantic relations between the different concepts entering into these phrases. The main ideas can be summarized as follows:

(a) Two phrases, in the same or different languages, having equivalent meanings must have the same internal representation, even if their syntactic structures are very different.

(b) All the information implied in a phrase must be made explicit in the internal representation. Thus, "I went to three chemists' this morning" would generally lead the hearer to assume that I failed to get what I wanted at the first two, and this inference must be made part of the "meaning" of the phrase.

(c) Every action is expressed in terms of certain primitives: thus a primitive for "drink" could be "ingest", which would serve also for "swallow" and "eat". A schema is associated with every primitive and must be completed, at least partially, before the process of understanding starts.

The meaning of a phrase is represented by a schema, called the *conceptual dependency;* this comprises categories (or nodes of the network) of four kinds:
  (i)   PP (Picture Production): these are equivalent to nouns
  (ii) ACT (Action): these are equivalent to verbs or groups of verbs
  (iii) PA (Picture Aider): these modify the PPs and thus are equivalent to adjectives
  (iv) AA (Action Aider): these modify the ACTs and thus are equivalent to adverbs.

The dependencies or relations are:

$< = = >$: a mutual dependence between two concepts, showing that both are necessary. This occurs most frequently between a PP and an ACT

$<$————   : one-way dependence between an ACT and a PP (e.g. between verb and object) or between a PP and a PA

$< = =$: one-way dependence between two PPs, such as that of possession.

Thus the conceptual dependency schema for "Henry polished his new car" is:

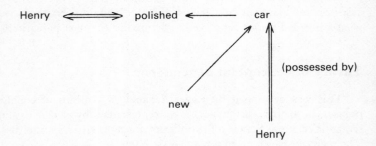

Figure 4.2   Henry polished his new car

For the distinction between conceptual-dependency representation and case-oriented grammar consider the phrase "John angered Henry". This would be represented in the grammar by the schema of Fig. 4.3.

Conceptual Dependency displays the causal relations, denoting these by ⋔. In this example "John" has performed an action which is not made explicit and which is expressed by DO, as a result of which Henry is in a state of anger. The representation is as in Fig. 4.4, where "P" indicates the past tense.

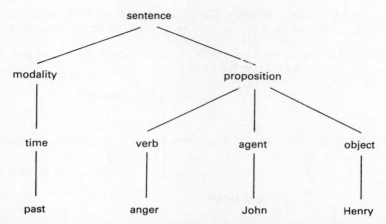

Figure 4.3 Case-oriented grammar representation of "John angered Henry"

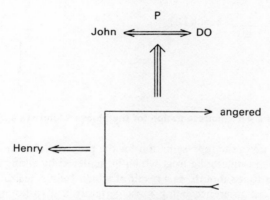

Figure 4.4 Representation in conceptual dependency of "John angered Henry"

Thus, to simplify the matter somewhat, the process of representing the meaning of a phrase consists in primitive or primitives corresponding to the actions and completing the associated structures. There are altogether 12—14 primitives, a few of which are given below.

ATRANS indicates the abstract concept of transfer of something to a person (e.g. GIVE), to oneself (e.g. TAKE) or the simultaneous transfer of several objects (e.g. BUY, which implies the transfer of goods and money).

PTRANS indicates physical transfer from one place to another, as in GO referring to oneself or PUT referring to an object.

MBUILD indicates a mental process of constructing new items of information from old, such as DECIDE, CONCLUDE, IMAGINE, DEDUCE, CONSIDER.

SPEAK   indicates production of sounds, e.g. SPEAK, SING, CRY.
ATTEND   indicates the use of a sense organ to detect a stimulus, e.g.
          HEAR, SEE.
EXPEL   indicates the expulsion of an object by an animal, e.g.
          BREATHE, CRY, SPIT.

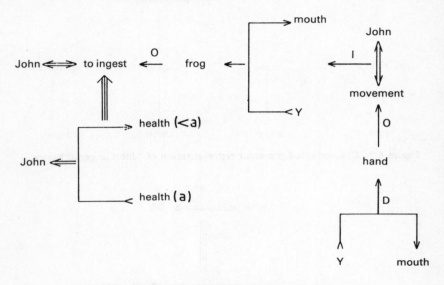

Figure 4.5   Representation for the phrase "John ate a frog"

Figure 4.5 gives the representation for the phrase "John ate a frog". This means that "John ingested a frog, which he achieved by taking it in his hand and carrying it to his mouth: as a result of which John's health will certainly suffer"—this last inference being most certainly a manifestation of Roger Schank's fundamental Francophobia!

Riesbeck's conceptual analyzer, which is used in the process of deriving such a representation, is strongly guided by the possible final representation which generates possible expectations. A version of this analyzer is presented in Chapter 5. Similar work has also been done by Wilks,[10] with his theory of preferential semantics.

Notes and references

[1] Winograd T. (1972), *Understanding Natural Language*, New York, Academic Press.

[2] Woods W., Kaplan R., Nash-Webber B. (1972), "The Lunar Sciences Natural Language System", *BBN final report*, Cambridge, Mass.

[3] Coulon D., Kayser D. (1980), "Un système de raisonnement à profondeur variable", *Congrès AFCET-TTI*, Nancy, pp. 517-527.

[4] Meehan J. R. (1976), "The metanovel: Writing stories by computer", *Ph. D thesis*, Yale University report No. 74.

[5] McDonald D. D. (1980), "Language production as a process of decision making under constraints", *Ph. D thesis*, MIT, Cambridge, Mass.

[6] Halliday M. A. K. (1970), "Language structure and language function", in *New Horizons in Linguistics*, John Lyons (ed.), Harmondsworth, England, Penguin Books.

[7] Schank R. C. (1975), *Conceptual Information Processing*, New York, North-Holland.

[8] Fillmore C. (1968), "The case for case", in Bach and Harms (eds.), *Universals in Linguistic theory*, Chicago, Holt, Rinehart and Winston.

[9] Schank R. C. (1972), "Conceptual Dependency: a theory of natural language understanding", *Cognitive Psychology*, 3.

[10] Wilks Y. (1975), "A preferential, pattern-seeking semantics for natural language inference", *Artificial Intelligence* 6, pp. 53-74.

5
Some Techniques for the Analysis of Natural Languages

This chapter deals with the following problem: given a phrase in some natural language—English, say—identify its constituents and the relationship between these so as to define a structure that will represent the meaning of the phrase in the internal form required by the computer. Here I am deliberately avoiding giving any firm definition of "meaning", and leaving unspecified whether the treatment is to go no further than identifying such concepts as subject, verb, complement, place of action and so on or whether, and above all, any inferences should be included. Schank and those who adopt his approach would include all the cognitive processes that are brought into play in the process of understanding.

These questions are taken up in more detail in the chapter on the understanding of text, Chapter 8; here we consider only the translation of natural language phrases into a form that can be represented inside a computer.

Recursive Transition Networks (RTNs)

The term denotes a method for specifying a grammar. RTNs are derived from finite-state automata, with some essential additions that enable the recursive nature of some definitions to be taken into account; so far as powers of expression are concerned they are equivalent to context-free grammars.

A finite-state automaton consists of a set of nodes, representing states, linked by arcs showing how one state may change into another. There is an initial state (START) and one or more final states (FINISH) and in the case of an RTN the arcs are labelled to indicate words or classes of words, meaning that the state change represented by an arc is made when a word is encountered that matches the label word, or is of the appropriate class if that is how the arc is labelled. We say that an automaton will *accept* a given sequence of words if it can take the first word as START and reach the last word as a FINISH. The automaton of Fig. 5.1 will accept the phrase "the pretty little pony", or just "the pony", but not "little pony".

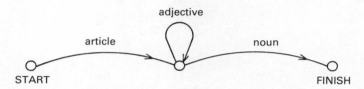

Figure 5.1   Finite-state automaton for a very simple noun phrase

Such an automaton could not give a recursive representation of a phrase of the type "the husband of the sister of the hallporter of the hotel", characterized by having an arbitrary number of prepositional groups. Nested clauses in natural-language statements can always be replaced by iterative structures, but the usual result of doing this is that the structure natural to the meaning suffers. The difficulty can be avoided by labelling the arcs not only with terminal symbols such as VERB or NOUN, which lead directly to the words of the language, but also by non-terminal symbols such as NG, PG meaning noun group and prepositional group respectively, which are in turn defined by further automata forming part of, and able to refer to, the complete system. This is the idea underlying the Recursive Transition Network (RTN) technique; Fig. 5.2 gives an RTN that will accept a phrase such as "the clever little daughter of the owner of the sweet-shop has won a scholarship to Oxford."

Here the terminal categories are: N (noun), V (verb), ADJ (adjective), PREP (preposition), DET (determinant). The non-terminal categories are: NG (noun group), PG (prepositional group). The fact that a NG can contain a PG, and vice versa, shows the importance of including the possibility of recursion in a programming language.

This is a very practical method for analyzing statements, but it does not allow us easily to take account of all the phenomena of natural language, and in particular of certain contextual aspects; although these can be dealt with by rather extravagant duplications of the specifications, as is illustrated below. In the analysis process, the path to be taken on leaving a node depends entirely on the route by which that node was reached. Suppose for example that we are looking at the verb in the phrase and wish to know if it agrees with the noun

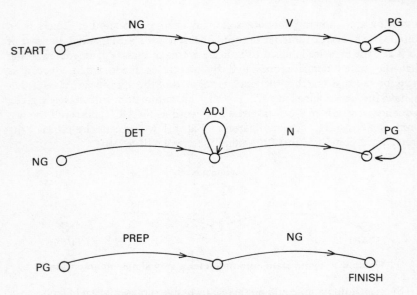

Figure 5.2   Example of Recursive Transition Network (RTN)

found in the noun group; this is a matter of concern for many language scholars, for the verb can often be understood in several different senses and the appropriate choice may depend, for example, on the nature of the noun—whether it denotes a living creature such as an animal or an inanimate object such as a table.

For the particular case of agreement in number, this can be ensured by means of a context-free grammar of the following form:

P : : Psing/Pplural
Psing : := NGsing/VGsing
Pplural : := NGplural/VGplural
NGsing : := DETsing/ADJsing/Nsing
etc.

but only at the cost of creating a very burdensome system.

Contextual aspects are handled much more neatly by the ATN system conceived by Woods,[1] which will be described next.

Augmented Transition Networks (ATNs)

These have the following three advantages over RTNs:

(i)   They allow any kind of test to be associated with the arcs, as well as the condition of having to belong to a stated syntactic or semantic class. Thus we could require that a NOUN should be of the same class as an ARTICLE found previously in the network, and consequently reject "table" or "telephone" as the subject of the verb "dream".

(ii) They allow us to specify actions to be followed if the branch is taken: for example, the storing of an item of information for later use.

(iii) They provide a set of registers for maintaining links between the various sub-networks of the complete system.

Woods has developed a standard vocabulary for describing a grammar in terms of the ATN formalism. There is, for example, an arc of type JUMP to allow transition from one state to the next without using the entry word. And there is also a standard means of taking account of main and relative clauses when there is a need to go back to the beginning of a phrase after a long interruption, as in "the boy whom I saw yesterday getting off a bus with a tall girl who had a red umbrella was the parson's son".

The ATN of Fig. 5.3 can understand the following questions:

1(a) Which is the ship of greatest length?
1(b) Which is the longest ship?
2(a) Which are the ships of greatest length?
2(b) Which are the longest ships?

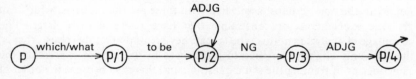

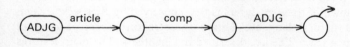

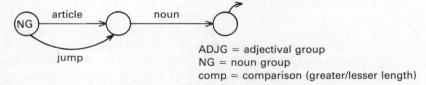

ADJG = adjectival group
NG = noun group
comp = comparison (greater/lesser length)

Figure 5.3 ATN for analysis of "Which is the longest ship?", etc.

The forms 1a and 1b have equivalent meanings, as do 2a and 2b; the difference between the two groups is signalled by setting the NUMBER register to SINGULAR or PLURAL as appropriate, after examining the words is (are), ship(s). This could be used for checking purposes, such as flagging as a grammatical error if someone typed the words "The ship are".

Analysis of queries

The programs used here are such that the set of acceptable phrases is not defined precisely by a set of rules, as would be the case if they were generated by a phrase-structure grammar, or by a graph in which the class of each word as it was encountered determined the branch to be taken next. Analyzers of this type do not generally examine every word of the sentence but concentrate on certain concepts, usually those associated with the verb. These are normally concerned with case, such as agent, object, instrument, etc., or modalities such as tense, which are searched for as soon as the verb has been identified. In this analysis the set of cases is associated not with the verb itself but with the appropriate primitive (see Chapter 4): thus in Conceptual Dependency Theory "ingest" is the primitive for "swallow", "eat", "drink", "ingurgitate", etc.

The most important words are the verbs, in the verbal groups, and the nouns, in the noun groups; associated with these are the requests, which can generate expectations or constraints that have to be satisfied later. The advantage of analyzers of this type is that they are undoubtedly robust, that is, they are only slightly sensitive to differences in the way of expressing the same idea or of framing the same question; and this is so because the order of the words is not of fundamental importance to the process. Thus in particular there is no need to foresee all the possible ways the same statement could be made; but on the other hand they do not generally enable account to be taken of any nuances that might have been expressed by the particular word order.

The best known of these analyzers is that conceived by Riesbeck,[2] which derives from a natural language phrase the structure corresponding to Conceptual Dependency Theory, described in Chapter 4. The main features of such analyzers are as follows:

1. They do not seek to build the syntactic structure of the phrase, but to find the meaning directly, in the context in which the phrase appears.
2. They use very little syntactic information.
3. They make little distinction between linguistic and non-linguistic inform- ation, but attach great importance to inferences and beliefs. The process of finding the semantic structure starts before the whole of the phrase has been read: Riesbeck maintains strongly that this is probably the way in which our own understanding of language operates.

The analyzer described below is Riesbeck's ELI[3] (English Language Interpreter). It has these characteristics:

(a) The dictionary consists of production rules (see Chapter 12) which perform the major part of the analysis.
(b) It uses constraints expressing conceptual dependencies, which it constructs so as to control the use of these rules.
(c) It produces schemas showing the conceptual dependencies.

There is a special type of production rule, called REQUEST; this has, in addition to the normal specifications of actions and conditions, extra fields such as FOCUS OF TEST and SUGGESTIONS, the latter enabling further tests to be specified, to be applied if this particular request is executed.

In general, the executing of a test contributes to the building of a syntactic–semantic structure and to establishing what information is needed in order to complete such a structure; for the latter, the attributes not yet specified are examined, usually those associated with the verb: for example, if the phrase to be analyzed is "John said to Ann that Robert would go", as soon as the verb "to say" (in the form "said") is identified this is used to enter the dictionary and as a result the appropriate entry is made in a structure in the form of Fig. 5.4. Here PERSON 1 is replaced by JOHN and completion of

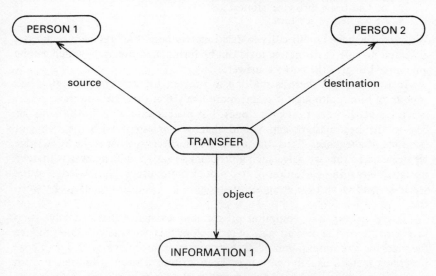

Figure 5.4 Partial structure expressing the fact that one person has transferred an item of information (about himself) to another

the rest of the structure left until the analysis has proceeded further. We can express this by saying that the structure has been *partially instantiated.*

There may be constraints to be satisfied in this process; here, for example,

PERSON 2 must be a "person", but INFORMATION 1 can be any complete concept, in this case "Robert would go".

As ELI reads the words input to the program it consults the dictionary, from which it extracts definitions which it passes on to the procedure INCORPORATE, resulting in a group of requests being loaded into the computer's memory. These are then examined by another procedure, CONSIDER, which executes those for which the CONDITION is satisfied and eliminates any that are inconsistent with other structures in the memory.

The problem of pronomial references

The problem is to find the correct noun to which a pronoun refers, and is one of the most difficult to solve in complete generality. Consider the following, adapted from an example given by Jacques Pitrat:[4]

The teacher sent the boy to the headmaster because
1. he had had enough of him;
2. he had been throwing stones;
3. he wanted to see him.

We ourselves have no difficulty in deciding to whom "he" refers in each case, although no rule in deductive logic can be formulated precisely which can be guaranteed to give the correct answer.

In this example there is nothing to prevent the boy from "having had enough of him", although it seems more likely that this refers to the teacher; nor the teacher from throwing stones, but in that case why did he send the boy to the headmaster? and would that be consistent with the behavior expected of a teacher? Thus the question that arises is, what is the knowledge we draw on so that we solve such a problem so easily? The answer is that we use a wide-ranging collection of items of "commonsense" knowledge of the world around us and are aware of sociological and political relations between these.

There are very few computer programs in existence that can solve such problems, for in the present state of technology it is extremely difficult to give the machine a representation of all these pieces of informal knowledge. Those programs that do usually work have been written with only limited aims in view and use fairly simple methods; one method is to take as the referent the noun or noun group last used in the phrase, another can be stated as follows: assign to each of the last n nouns a weight which initially is a decreasing function of its distance from the pronoun, and increase this weight whenever a semantic link with the noun is found.

The problem of conjunctions and elliptic constructions

The use of conjunctions, which is a very convenient way of condensing two clauses or avoiding repetition of a part of a phrase, can give rise to very subtle problems in the analysis of natural-language statements. For example:

Paul and John came to dinner.
James played the violin and Ann the piano.

Similarly, problems arise from elliptic constructions, in which a part of a phrase is suppressed and is to be taken as implied:

What is the capital of Germany? Of Mexico?

One's first idea of how to deal with the conjunction problem is this: whenever a conjunction is found, try to find if the succeeding phrase is at least partially consistent with a recently-used grammatical rule. Thus in the above example:

(and) "Ann the piano"

is partly consistent with the structure:

noun   verb   article   noun

which is that of

"James played the violin"

and the verb is missing. But unfortunately there are usually very many possibilities, and these cannot be eliminated except by semantic criteria or on grounds of commonsense; and there can be essential ambiguities, as in

parking reserved for senior managers and directors

where it is not clear whether all directors may park there, or only senior ones.

An even greater difficulty results from different use of words which act as logical operators in natural language on the one hand and in information processing on the other. Thus consider this simple natural-language query:

How many personal computers did we sell in North and South Carolina?

If this is to be expressed in a formal language acceptable to a database query program the last part, defining the sales region of interest, can be expressed in any of the four forms

1. REGION = NORTH AND SOUTH CAROLINA
2. REGION = NORTH OR SOUTH CAROLINA
3. REGION = NORTH CAROLINA OR SOUTH CAROLINA
4. REGION = NORTH CAROLINA AND SOUTH CAROLINA

The only correct form is (3), because (4) implies a contradiction—no region can be simultaneously North Carolina and South Carolina. The point is that the conjunctions AND and OR do not have the same sense in formal logic as they do in ordinary language.

There are good accounts of the problems of analysis of natural language in the books by Terry Winograd[5] and Wendy Lehnert.[6]

Conclusion

There are many unresolved problems in the analysis of natural language. Apart from the complexity of framing the rules of a formal grammar which will allow any phrases to be generated that are acceptable as natural language, there is the reasonable question of whether there would be any value in doing so, because we are able to understand many ungrammatical phrases. Further, the richness of a natural language, a consequence of the many senses in which its words can be understood and of the ambiguities which give the language much of its beauty, will for long remain a major challenge to the development of methods for representing knowledge of the real world.

Notes and references

[1] Woods, W. (1970), "Transition network programs for natural language analysis", *CACM 13* 10, pp. 591-606.
[2] Riesbeck, C. K. (1975), "Conceptual analysis" in *Conceptual information processing*, Schank (ed.), New York, North Holland.
[3] Riesbeck, C. K. (1978), "An expectation-driven production system for natural language understanding" in *Pattern-directed inference systems*, Waterman and Hayes-Roth (eds.) New York, Academic Press.
[4] Pitrat, J. (1978), "La programmation informatique du language", *La Recherche* No. 93.
[5] Winograd, T. (1982), *Language as a cognitive process*, Reading, Mass., Addison-Wesley.
[6] Lehnert, W. and Ringle, M. (1982), (eds.), *Strategies for natural language processing*. Hillsdale, N.J., Lawrence Erlbaum.

6
Understanding Speech:
Some Aspects
of the Problem

A constant concern of AI researchers is the development of "friendly" interfaces between information processing systems and their users: for example, for gaining access to a database. Since speech is one of our most natural methods of communication, many workers have been drawn into the field of speech understanding and synthesis. This chapter deals only with the problem of understanding speech, which is the more difficult; the reader interested in speech synthesis should consult, for example, Witten (1982).[1]

Understanding speech is a more difficult problem than understanding written (or typed) natural language for several reasons, of which the following are the main ones:

(a) The speech signal contains "noise", that is, sounds that carry no information and must be eliminated.
(b) Pronunciation is not perfect and varies from one speaker to another.
(c) The pronunciation of a single speaker varies from one time to another, depending on his psychological and physiological state.
(d) The pronunciation of a phoneme or of a word can vary according to whether it is spoken in isolation or with other words.
(e) There are no clear boundaries in the vocal signal between successive words; there can be intervals of silence in the middle of a word, or absence of any interval between successive words.
(f) Words of entirely different spellings and meanings can have identical pronunciations—the problem of homonyms: for example, right, rite, write; pair, pare, pear.

The consequence is that the input to a system intended for understanding speech is a web of phonetic elements representing the transcription of the sentence originally spoken; this will contain many errors—of the order of 30% at best, at present—which leads to a significant degree of indefiniteness in the subsequent processing.

Starting with this web of sounds, a web of words can be extracted by all the combinations that are allowable in that particular context. The task of the analyzer could then be to find a coherent path through this web of words, using whatever information was available. This purely bottom-up process, however, proves inadequate for languages of above a low level of complexity and has to be complemented by a top-down process, guided by semantic, syntactic, pragmatic and other information at a higher level.

It is primarily the problem of recognizing isolated words that is tackled by present-day equipment. This is a much simpler problem than that of recognizing continuous speech, but even here, according to Lea,[2] although the best systems have a success rate of 99.5% they only attain this with a vocabulary of the order of 120 words spoken by a single trained speaker. Devices for recognizing sequences of words, spoken continuously and having no syntactic structure, have been in operation for several years.

Levels of recognition

If the starting point is the sound signal then, according to Barr,[3] the process of achieving full understanding of what was spoken depends on the following types of knowledge being provided.

(a) *Phonetic:* representation of the characteristics of all the sounds occurring in the words of the vocabulary.

(b) *Phonological:* rules giving the variations in pronunciation when the words are spoken in phrases; these concern the phenomena of co-articulation, assimilation, etc.

(c) *Morphemic:* rules stating how the morphemes (the smallest meaningful units) can be combined so as to make the words; these include rules for formation of plurals, conjugation of verbs, etc.

(d) *Prosodic:* rules describing the variations in accent and intonation, such as the rising tone at the end of a question.

(e) *Syntactic:* rules governing the formation of phrases.

(f) *Semantic:* ways in which various words and phrases can be used to eliminate constructions that are syntactically correct but are unlikely to occur.

(g) *Pragmatic:* rules applying to conversations, enabling, for example, the speaker's intentions to be anticipated and a response made that is more appropriate to the situation than a low-level interpretation.

The great difficulty in understanding speech arises from two sources of error and uncertainty that are inherent in the process, one due to the speaker and the other to the hearer. The speaker, in translating his thoughts into sounds, will make mistakes such as choosing the wrong words and pronouncing them wrongly or not clearly enough, repeat words unnecessarily, make curious and meaningless sounds such as clearing his throat, and introduce other individual peculiarities that corrupt the message. The hearer has to perform the inverse transformation to that of the speaker, going from the corrupted signal to the speaker's intentions; and makes mistakes that are errors of judgment, because there are no precise rules governing understanding. It is a common observation that communication between humans is accompanied by many requests for repetition and clarification.

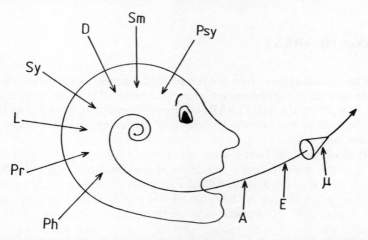

Figure 6.1 Some of the mechanisms that affect the vocal message (*from Newell*[4])
Psy psychology of the speaker, Sm semantics, D rules governing discourse, Sy syntax, L lexical considerations, Pr prosodic considerations, Ph phonetics, A the speaker's sound-producing apparatus, E environmental noise, μ microphone

Some speech-recognition programs

A five-year program (1971-1976) of research into the recognition of continuous speech was financed by the US Department of Defense Advanced Research Project Agency (ARPA). The aim was to produce computer programs capable of analyzing correctly-constructed phrases built with a vocabulary of about a thousand words and always concerning some limited field of interest; and to have an error rate of at most 10%. In this project the firm Bolt Beranek and Newman (BBN) developed first SPEECHLIS and then HWIM,[5] Carnegie-Mellon University developed different versions of HEARSAY[6] and HARPY,[7] and SRI International, in collaboration with System Development Corporation, developed the program SRI/SDC.[8] Extensions to another program, called DRAGON, were made by IBM[9] and other work was done at Bell Labs.

Work in France on this problem resulted in the development of a number of systems: MYRTILLE-I and -II[10,11] at CRIN (Centre de Recherche en Informatique de Nancy); ESOPE[12] at LIMSI (Laboratoire d'Informatique et de Mécanique pour les Sciences de l'Ingénieur), Orsay; KEAL[13] at CNET (Centre National d'Etude des Télécommunications), Lannion; a system at the University of Marseille[14]; and another at ENSER Grenoble.[15]

Project HEARSAY

This system operates in a non-hierarchical manner, which means that the various sources of supplementary information listed above (phonetic, etc.) are used independently. HEARSAY-II uses a "blackboard model", so called because each source records the result of its action, erases a result now obsolete, and so on.

Starting from the lowest level, a sequence of levels is identified in the course of the analysis: first a separation of the signal into segments, then a syllabic level at which possible syllables are assigned to the acoustic segments, and then an organizing of the syllables into words. Above this, at the top level, the sources of syntactic and semantic information are used. The program was tested with spoken chess moves, a field which is limited semantically but which nevertheless allows very general methods of representation of the signals to be tested.

The general architecture of HEARSAY allows a number of independent sources of information to co-operate in the solution of the problem; it has been used in fields other than speech recognition, for example in air traffic control. From this point of view the version HEARSAY-II is often regarded as an "expert system"—a subject dealt with in Chapter 15.

Project MYRTILLE

MYRTILLE-I and -II were developed at CRIN, University of Nancy. MYRTILLE-I can recognize very limited phrases in artificial languages, using a vocabulary of less than 100 words; it is a purely top-down system, syntactically driven. MYRTILLE-II has been applied in the field of meteorology, with a vocabulary of 375 words and a syntax quite close to that of spoken French; it uses a combined bottom-up and top-down strategy, as do most systems of this degree of complexity. It can start the analysis of a phrase from several base points, using a method similar to that of the "islands of confidence" used in HWIM; this is described in the following section of this chapter.

Here are English translations of some phrases with which MYRTILLE-II can deal:

When will the temperature rise?
When will it freeze in Lorraine?
Will it rain in the Nancy region?
Will there be less risk of icy roads in the Metz region tomorrow?

Control strategies

There is much greater variation between the methods used by the many speech-recognition systems now developed for controlling the use of their knowledge bases than there is between the types of knowledge that are used: the different types, listed on page 54, always range from the phonetic to the semantic and pragmatic.

In HARPY the sounds are represented by the nodes of a pre-compiled graph as in the ATNs of Chapter 5, the arcs representing possible ways in which these sounds could be linked to form syllables or words; thus the process of interpreting a phrase consists in finding a possible continuous path through the graph. This gives the system an integrated type of architecture which is not easy to modify but which was judged to be the most efficient in term of computer time of all those developed in the 1971-1976 ARPA project. HARPY analyzes its phrases from left to right using a fan-out strategy, which is not necessarily the best strategy when the start of the phrase has not been recognized with certainty.

A more sophisticated strategy, but one which is more difficult to incorporate, uses as base points segments of the phrase which have been recognized with some confidence—the "islands of confidence" previously referred to, or "best-recognized islands"—and conducts the analysis from one "island" to the next, either left to right or right to left. MYRTILLE-II and SRI/SDC use this method. The risk of having to examine a large number of possibilities can usually be reduced by strategies that focus attention on the subject being discussed, selecting at the semantic level the words that are most likely to be spoken. A hybrid between this and the HARPY strategy is used in HWIM, which attempts to recognize one word or another in a group of three or four, continuing the analysis in the two directions starting from the word that has been sufficiently well recognized.

Conclusion

At present, the performance of speech-recognition systems is markedly inferior to that of systems for understanding written (or typed) natural language. The main reason for this lies in the uncertainties resulting from the imperfections of the decoding of the speech signal. The error rate here could, in theory, be reduced by using semantic or pragmatic information concerning the subject of the message. This requires that the field of interest is limited or that a closed world can be assumed. If this assumption can in fact be made, the consequential possibility of making confident predictions about what will be said next reduces the range of the phonetic hypotheses that have to be considered. However, this type of interaction between different levels of understanding is not easy to implement.

More generally, decoding would be improved by a better formalization of items of phonetic information and their integration into the recognition systems.

Notes and references

[1] Witten, J. H. (1982), *Principles of computer speech*, New York, Academic Press.
[2] Lea W. (1980), *Trends in speech recognition*, Englewood Cliffs, N. J., Prentice-Hall.
[3] Barr A., Feigenbaum E. A. (1982), *The AI handbook*, vol. 1, Kaufmann, (ed.), Los Altos, California.
[4] Newell A. (1975), "A Tutorial on Speech Understanding Systems", in *Speech recognition: Invited papers of the IEEE Symposium*, D. R. Reddy (ed.), New York, Academic Press.
[5] Wolf J., Woods W. (1980), "The HWIM Speech Understanding System", in Lea, *Trends*, pp. 316-339.
[6] Erman L. D., Hayes-Roth F., Lesser V. R., Reddy D. R. (1980), "The Hearsay-II Speech Understanding System: Integrating knowledge to resolve uncertainty", *Computing Surveys*, vol. 12, no. 2.
[7] Lowerre B., Reddy R. (1980), "The HARPY Speech Understanding System", in Lea, *Trends*, pp. 340-360.
[8] Walker D. (ed.) (1980), *Understanding spoken language*, New York, North-Holland.
[9] Bahl L. R., et al. (1978), "Automatic recognition of continuously spoken sentences from a finite state grammar". *Proc. of the 1978 IEEE International Conference on Acoustics, Speech and Signal Processing*, Tulsa, Oklahoma.

[10] Haton J. P., Messenet G., Pierrel J. M., Sanchez C. (1978), "La Chaîne de compréhension parlée du système MYRTILLE-II, *Congrès AFCET-TTI,* Paris.

[11] Pierrel J. M. (1982), "Utilisation de contraintes linguistiques en compréhension automatique de la parole continue: le système MYRTILLE-II", *Revue RAIRO/TSI,* vol. 1, no. 5, pp. 403-421.

[12] Mariani J. J. (1982), "The AESOP continuous speech understanding system", *IEEE-ICASSP,* pp. 1637-1640.

[13] Mercier G., Gérard M. (1981), "Les niveaux acoustique-phonétique et l'apprentissage dans le système KEAL", *JEP GALF.*

[14] Meloni H. (1982), "Étude et réalisation d'un système de reconnaissance automatique de la parole continue", *Thèse de doctorat d'Etat,* Université d'Aix-Marseille 2, Luminy.

[15] Groc B., Tuffelli D. (1980), "A continuous Speech recognition system for database consultation", *IEEE-ICASSP,* Denver, Co., pp. 896-899.

7
Friendly Interfaces in Natural Language

Introduction

It is often advantageous to be able to communicate in a natural language with a database or an expert system; a typical case is that of the user who is not a computer specialist and who has little enthusiasm for learning an artificial programming language with its rigid syntax and a logic that is likely to conflict with his way of expressing his needs. Another is the occasional user—possibly also a non-expert—on whom it is out of the question to impose an artificial syntax because he or she will forget the rules between sessions. A further reason for providing a natural-language interface is that the user is unlikely to be familiar with the details of the structure of the database and that the access program must therefore be able to perform at least some minimum amount of interpretation of a request. There is, however, the danger with such an interface that the user may come to credit the program with more intelligence than it actually possesses, and thus think that it is able to make interpretations and inferences that are in fact beyond its capacity. The user may then suffer a loss of interest when the program's limitations become apparent.

There are many examples of top managerial staff who have terminals on their desks which they seldom use, simply because too little attention has been paid to making the system "friendly". The very common menu-driven systems are often tedious to use because they require the users to work down through a deep tree structure when they would much prefer to express their needs directly in a familiar language.

Interfaces at different levels

The main purpose of an interface is to hide from the user the technical details of the system with which he or she is communicating, for example the way in which a database is structured; and in general its method of working is to transform the request as expressed by the user, in a form that the user finds natural, into the formal expression required by the search program.

Two levels of development of interfaces can be considered. Interfaces at the first level already exist as research and development projects and are beginning to be incorporated into commercial products; those at the second level are still the subject of research and will not become generally available for some years yet.

Level 1: these enable queries of the following types to be made.

(i) Those which require no inferences to be made: for example, In what country is Madrid?

(ii) Those for which some inference has to be made or which require some computation: for example, How long does it take by train to get from Brooklyn to Philadelphia? It is unlikely that sufficient information would be held so that any such question could be answered directly; but it is likely that the distance between any pair of towns could be found or computed and hence, from a knowledge of the average speed of trains, an approximate time could be given.

(iii) Queries about the information held in the database: What items of information does the base contain? What is there about the employees of such-and-such a company? We may call such information "meta-knowledge".

Examples of systems operating at this level are ROBOT/INTELLECT,[1] LADDER,[2] SAPHIR.[3]

Level 2: the following extensions to the abilities of the Level 1 interfaces should appear during the next few years.

(a) "Intelligent" replies to "stupid" questions, such as, Which is the shortest river in England? For how many days in 1983 was the temperature above 150°C? The first of these makes no sense because the set of English river lengths is semi-open—closed at the upper limit (the length of the longest river is known) but open at the lower (it is very likely that there is a river of shorter length than the smallest length recorded); and in any event, the fact of being short is of little interest in connection with rivers. Collins[4] has studied this problem in detail.

Most systems would respond to the second question by scanning the daily temperature records for 1983 and giving the answer "none"; but as Daniel Kayser[5] has remarked, we ourselves would not apply the same reasoning to this question as we would if the temperature quoted were 25°C—that is, we should use our meta-knowledge.

(b) Concise statements instead of, and more informative than, detailed lists. Thus if the question is, Who in the organization has a company car? the reply "The president and the vice-presidents" is much more informative than a list of names.

(c) Replies that show some spirit of co-operation with the enquirer rather than being merely literally correct. This is illustrated by the following sequence of questions and replies conceived by Kaplan:[6]

Q1: Which students got more than 15% in the biology examination in June 1983?
R1: None.
Q2: Were there any failures in biology in June 1983?
R2: No.
Q3: How many students passed in biology in June 1983?
R3: None
Taken aback by this reply, the questioner decides to put a further question:
Q4: Was there a biology examination in June 1983?
R4: No. (a reply that could have been given at the start).

An interface-building tool: LIFER

A good example of a tool for building a natural-language interface to a database or expert system is LIFER[7] developed at SRI International. This consists of an interpreter for the rules of a grammar, together with a set of very useful editing functions to help the user specify the grammatical rules he wishes to impose. It is used mainly for putting questions in natural language; each grammatical rule consists of a template specifying the syntactic form of an input question and an output template giving the form in which this is to be transmitted to the database; here we are interested only in the first.

The process of developing an interface consists in first defining a set of productions at the top level and then specifying the categories of objects that can appear at successively lower levels, finishing with the words that form the vocabulary of the domain of interest. Figure 7.1 gives the syntactic tree for the question, put to a naval database, "When will Bravo's sonar be operational?"

A *category* can be defined in several ways:

1. By a list of its possible values, given explicitly: e.g.

   <ANIMAL> : : = (DOG / CAT / HORSE)

2. By a predicate, whose truth value has to be tested. This is important when the set of values is infinite but can be defined by some characteristic

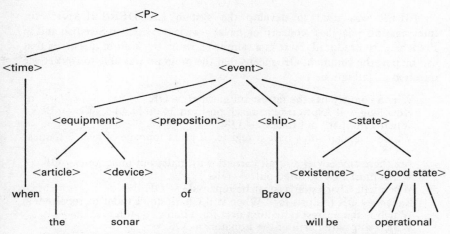

Figure 7.1   Syntactic tree for "When will Bravo's sonar be operational?"

property such as a number being integral. Another important case is when the condition for belonging to the category is relatively complex and is expressed by means of a program segment, which in effect constitutes the predicate.

3. Recursively, by a sequence of categories.

One of LIFER's qualities is the ability to deal with elliptical constructions, at least to some extent. This concerns incomplete questions where there is an implied reference to the preceding question, as in the following sequence; here UNDERSTOOD! means that the program has "understood" the question. The question is in lower case and the system's reply in capitals.

> What is John Smith's salary?
> UNDERSTOOD!
> ID 10324 SALARY 15500
> (The system gives the employee's personnel number as well as salary)
> Jack Robinson's?
> UNDERSTOOD!
> ID 31416 SALARY 28750

LIFER also allows the user to define expressions and give synonyms interactively, without any need to know how the database is structured in the machine; the program extends the dictionary automatically. For example:

> Let "honorarium" be a new name for "salary"
> UNDERSTOOD!
> What is James Joyce's honorariom?
> HONORARIOM ← HONORARIUM (corrects spelling)
> UNDERSTOOD!
> ID 271828 SALARY 5000

LIFER was used to develop the system LADDER/INLAND[2] for interrogating a database concerning naval vessels; versions in Swedish and in French[8] were produced. Here is a sample showing the kind of questions that can be put; the comment OK means that the program was able to answer the question unambiguously.

Which country has the fastest submarine? — OK
How long will Aspro take to reach position 34-00 N 43-15W? — OK
When will Shark put to sea? — OK
Which Angolan ships have a registered gross tonnage of over 5 tonnes?
— OK
Are there any Soviet aircraft carriers with radar out of action? — OK
When must Fox be fitted out? — OK
When will Charleston's sonar be repaired? — OK
Radar? — OK (ellipsis for "When will Charleston's radar be repaired?")
Which is the nearest refuelling port for Titanic? — OK
Which ships are north of the Equator? — OK
South of 12-56 N? (ellipsis for "Which ships are south of 12-56 N?")
British? — FAIL (the method for handling ellipsis fails here because "British" does not have the same structure as "south of position . . ."; the question is ambiguous and could mean either
        Which are the British ships?
or Which British ships are south of 12-56 N?)
Are there any ships over 333 metres? — OK
Cruising at over 12 knots? — OK (ellipsis for "Are there any ships . . . knots?")
Which ships are sailing under the Liberian flag? — OK
Expected at Le Havre? — OK (ellipsis for "Which ships are expected at Le Havre?")
NB The method for handling ellipsis sets up a correspondence between two verbal groups, and therefore the program does not consider the question of which Liberian ships are expected at le Havre.
Give me the draught and length of Fox. — OK
What is the name of the officer commanding Aspro? — OK
What is the loxodrome course from San Diego to Gibraltar? — OK
How far is Fox from Fall River? — OK
Which Zulu-5 class tanker is north of the Equator? — OK
When does Nautilus leave Venezela? — correction — Venezuela? — OK
Will Gato need revictualling in the next two days? — OK
When will Adroit be ready for service? — OK
Which is its home port? — OK
How many ships in the Mediterranean have a doctor on board? — OK

Among other programs having a natural-language interface to a database is PLANES,[9] corresponding to the above for the case of aircraft.

Programs of this type are not robust in all circumstances: they work well with questions put in a natural, straightforward and unambiguous manner but their performance deteriorates rapidly when the questions are imprecise or ambiguous or when the user sets out deliberately to trip the program. Thus a natural way to put a question is

How did Franklin Roosevelt die?

whilst a much less natural way is

Is the reason for the death of Franklin Roosevelt known?

and a very much less straightforward way is

Why did Franklin Roosevelt kick the bucket?

There is no theoretical limit to the complexity of the phrases that a human will accept, nor to their poetic level; any question can be put in a vast number of different ways and it is virtually impossible, in the present state of the art, to foresee, and program for, all the choices available to the user.

Some immediate possibilities

Several further applications of the techniques for understanding natural languages are already possible; the following list has been given by Waltz.[10]
1. Assistance in translation from one language to another; the machine's translation still needs to be looked over by a human, to resolve ambiguities and to improve the style.
2. The ability to "understand" a document and to make a précis, from which a reader can quickly decide whether or not it contains information he is seeking. Present-day systems reach only a modest level of understanding in cases where the material can concern any subject without restriction, and often perform little more than keyword searches.
3. Help in preparation of papers by taking over much of the work of an experienced editor, such as picking up errors in spelling and grammar and suggesting rephrasings so as to improve the quality of the text.
4. Generating documents, by turning information stored in a formal language into natural-language text; the style could be adapted to suit any particular class of reader.
5. Applications such as the control of access to large databases, control of industrial robots, provision of precisely-expressed information and advice in special fields (medical, legal, etc.) by means of expert systems.

Notes and references

[1] Harris L. (1977), "ROBOT, a high performance natural language data base query system", *IJCAI-77*, pp. 903-904.
[2] Sacerdoti, E. D. (1977), "Language access to distributed data with error recovery", *IJCAI-77*, Cambridge, Mass.

[3] Erli (1983), "SAPHIR, présentation générale", *Rapport de la Société d'Etude et de Recherche en Linguistique et Informatique.*

[4] Collins A., Warnock E. H., Aiello N., Miller M. L. (1975), "Reasoning from incomplete knowledge", in *Representation and Understanding*, Bobrow and Collins (eds.), New York, Academic Press.

[5] Kayser D. (1984), "Examen de diverses méthodes utilisées en représentation des connaissances", *4e Congrès d'Intelligence Artificielle et Reconnaissance des Formes*, Paris.

[6] Kaplan S. J. (1982), "Cooperative responses from a portable natural language query system", *Artificial Intelligence*, Vol. 19, 2, pp. 165-188.

[7] Hendrix G. (1977), The LIFER manual: "A guide to building practical natural language interfaces". Technical note 138, *SRI International*, Menlo Park, California.

[8] Bonnet A. (1980), "Les grammaires sémantiques, outil puissant pour interroger les bases de données en langage naturel", *RAIRO Informatique/Computer Science*, Vol. 14, 2, pp. 137-148.

[9] Waltz D., Goodman B. (1977), "Writing a natural language data base system", *IJCAI-77*, pp. 144-150, MIT Press, Cambridge, Mass.

[10] Waltz D. (1983), "Artificial Intelligence: an assessment of the state-of-the art and recommendations for future directions", *AI Magazine*, Fall 1983, pp. 55-67.

8
Understanding Text

Introduction

In the period to which Chapter 7 relates, the orientation of research was towards the understanding of isolated phrases. This raised several problems: for one thing it is only rarely that we as humans have to analyze phrases out of all context, and for another we often give indirect replies to questions put to us. Consider for example the following dialog:

Q: Where is the photocopier?
R: It's broken.

Clearly, the person questioned assumed that the questioner wanted to use the photocopier—an inference that would probably be right, but not certainly so—and knew that in the event he would not be able to do so; so to reply that it was broken was likely to be more useful than to give a direct reply such as "In room 508".

Interest in analyzing isolated phrases is declining gradually. Some researchers are becoming interested in the causal relations in a text that give it a narrative sense, and in the motivations of the participants in the action, without which it is difficult to understand what is happening. These researches are developing in two phases:

First, attention will be directed to the structure of a narrative, with the development of a "story grammar" and the idea of a "script".

Second, the foci of interest will be the motivations of the participants and especially the ways in which these participants develop their plans so as to achieve certain ends.

Story grammars

This idea derives from the observation that most stories have a structure consisting of a series of episodes, just as a phrase consists of a series of syntactic groups. Rumelhart,[1] following Propp,[2] has concentrated on fairytales; these have, mostly, a rather simple structure: first an introduction of the personalities ("Once upon a time there was . . ."), then an account of an important event ("One day, when he was walking on the river bank . . .") which sets the machinery of the plot in motion, leading to the dénouement and a moral.

Two comments may be made on this method of attacking the problem. First, it is limited to very simple structures; and second, the part of the text that belongs to the category < verbal group > is more easily identified than that belonging to the category < moral >. So far as I know, there is no existing program that works in this way.

Scripts

It is clear that a program such as MARGIE, described in Chapter 4, will make a large number of inferences that fall outside the context of the material under consideration; and in fact the difficulty of limiting this number brings a risk of the process being defeated by the combinatorial explosion. Some limitation, and hence a partial solution to the problem, is provided by the use of *scripts* to link successive phrases together and impose constraints such as causal relations.

The idea of a script was introduced by Roger Schank and Robert Abelson.[3] It consists of a standard sequence of events that characterize some commonly-arising situation such as a visit to the cinema, to a restaurant or to the hairdresser; this concept is very close to that of the "frame" originated by Marvin Minsky, which is described in Chapter 13. Part of the RESTAURANT script is given in Fig. 8.1.

The essential point made by Schank and Abelson is that a knowledge of the scripts for many situations is necessary for the understanding of the way in which the different actions in any story are interlinked. Scripts describe the causal relations between the different episodes and make it possible to draw inferences, to guess things that are implied but not stated and to some extent fill in the blank spaces, so to speak, in the story as told—just as a human reader does, and with the same risk of error.

The part of the RESTAURANT script given in Fig. 8.1 is a general setting of the scene; the remainder consists of a number of main episodes: the entry of the customer(s), the giving of the order, the meal, paying the bill and

Accessories
Tables, menu, dishes, money, cheques, . . .

Participants
Customers, waiters/waitresses, cashier, manager, cook

Conditions of entry
Customer is hungry
Customer has money

Outcome
Customer has less money
Customer is no longer hungry
Customer is happy (possibly)
Manager has more money

Figure 8.1   Main lines of RESTAURANT script

leaving. The "order" episode has three sub-scenarios to suit different initial conditions, and so on . . . .

The SAM program

This was produced by Roger Schank and his colleagues at Yale;[4] the name stands for Script Applier Mechanism. It can "understand" narrative accounts such as the following.

"Last Friday evening a car ran off the M6 motorway after hitting the central barrier. The passenger, Francis Drake, of Warrington, was killed instantly according to the doctor, Dr. Lewis Pastor. The driver, Andrew Marvell, of 59 Middle Street, Lancaster, was taken to hospital by the rescue service and was allowed to go home after two days. No charges will be made. Police Inspector Sexton Blake is investigating the circumstances of the accident."

Given this text, the program produced the following summary:

"Four days ago a car hit the central barrier on M6. Francis Drake, living in Warrington, was killed. The driver, Andrew Marvell, of 59 Middle Street, Lancaster, was slightly injured. The police are making no charges."

It produced also a summary in Spanish:

"Un auto chocó contra la barrera central de la carretera M6 el viernes al anochecer . . ."

and was able to answer questions concerning the incident, as follows.

1. Was anyone killed?
   Yes, Francis Drake was killed.

2. Was anyone injured?
   Yes, Andrew Marvell was slightly injured.
3. Why was Andrew Marvell injured?
   Because the car hit the central barrier.
4. Was Andrew Marvell taken to hospital?
   Yes, he was taken to hospital.
5. How was Marvell taken to hospital?
   The rescue service took Marvell to hospital.

The SAM program uses the script CAR ACCIDENT together with various sub-scripts such as AMBULANCE; it is the latter that enables the deduction to be made that Andrew Marvell was slightly injured, a statement that is not contained in the original text, by establishing certain causal relations, particularly that between "the car struck the barrier" and "the driver was injured"—a commonsense inference.

An important point is that in produing the summary the program not only extracts the essential elements but also transforms the various phrases rather than simply reproducing the original text. In fact, SAM translates these into an internal representation which is independent of the superficial form of the language and from which it can generate summaries in different natural languages, as for example the Spanish version.

The BAOBAB program

BAOBAB[5,6] was developed around the medical expert system MYCIN (see Chapter 16) and uses the knowledge base of this to analyze medical histories written by doctors in a quasi-natural language. It is fairly typical of current research on the structure of dialog in that it is based on the assumption that the doctors express these histories in a stereotyped form; each history can be broken into a connected sequence of episodes and the understanding is very greatly helped by a knowledge of this structure.

The level of the program's ability to understand is indicated by its capacity for performing the following tasks:

— Suggesting that certain information is lacking
— Making inferences
— Checking for consistency
— Where necessary, interrupting the user to ask, for example, for clarific-
  ation of certain points
— Conducting a dialog in natural language in order to achieve an aim,
  with the analysis program using a semantic-type grammar.

Figure 8.2 shows the model of the world as known to BAOBAB, in the form of a sequence of schemas. Each schema is a data structure involving parameters of three types: those that are essential and must be given, those that are important but not essential and those that can be of auxiliary help. This hierarchy enables the program to interrupt the doctor if an essential parameter has not been given or if it seems that there has been a change of schema with little likelihood of returning to the previous one.

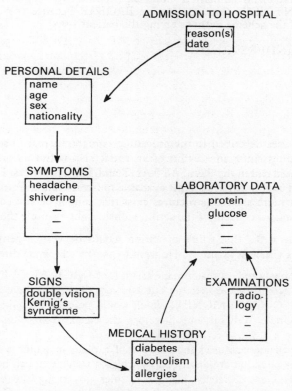

Figure 8.2   BAOBAB model of medical record

The following is an example of a dialog between BAOBAB and a doctor; the program's side is in capitals and the doctor's in lower case, following the double asterisks.

GOOD MORNING
** reasons for admission: shivering, headaches, nausea
SYMPTOMS NOTED
** date of admission: 25 December 1978
I UNDERSTAND THAT:
PATIENT ENTERED HOSPITAL FOUR DAYS AGO (inference from the date)

** Annie is West Indian and 26
I UNDERSTAND THAT:
PATIENT NAME IS ANNIE
PATIENT AGE IS 26
PATIENT NATIONALITY IS WEST INDIAN
(nationality could influence probability of certain diseases)
** the day before admission Annie experienced shivering and headaches
PATIENT SEX? (interruption by BAOBAB because the doctor has
changed the schema without giving the patient's sex)
** female
OK, I UNDERSTAND . . .

"Plans"

The analyses described in the preceding paragraphs make use of one or
more standard scripts; an account of an event in a railway dining car, for
example, would call in the RESTAURANT and TRAIN scripts. However, it
is clearly impossible to have scripts available to cover every eventuality and it
is likely that more abstract structures exist that cannot be embedded in the
relatively standard concept of the script. Consider for example the following:

"John knew that his wife's operation would be very expensive. Well,
there was Uncle William . . . He went to get the telephone directory . . ."

There is not likely to be a ready-made script for SURGICAL OPERATION,
because that would be too specific; but it is very likely that there is a general
plan HOW TO RAISE MONEY, which would point to the possibility of a
loan from Uncle William and therefore the need to find his telephone
number.

Schank's group has used the concept of a plan, in which a number of
possible lines of action are described by which a stated aim can be achieved.
In his thesis Gérard Sabah[7] has given rules governing the behavior of
characters in a story so as to explain their aims and their actions. Other uses of
the concept are given in Chapter 14, in particular in connection with chess.

We as humans use plans to understand sequences of phrases that,
superficially, are unrelated; consider the following, taken from Robert
Wilensky's account of his program PAM (Plan Applier Mechanism):[8]

Juliet was hungry.
She reached for the Michelin guide.

The second phrase is meaningful only insofar as it plays a part in outlining
the plan of action that can be inferred from the first. Schank has commented
that if the second phrase were replaced by "She reached for the Introduction
to Artificial Intelligence" this would have seemed extremely odd.

The following is a story handled by PAM:

John needed money. He took a gun and went into a shop. He told the shopkeeper to hand over his money. The shopkeeper gave the money and John left.

PAM was able to answer questions on this text; here is a sample.

why did John take a gun?
BECAUSE HE WANTED TO ROB THE SHOP
why did the shopkeeper give John the money?
BECAUSE HE DID NOT WANT TO BE WOUNDED
why did John leave?
BECAUSE HE DID NOT WANT TO BE CAUGHT

PAM's abilities come, in this case, from its knowledge of a plan HOW TO RAISE MONEY; given this goal, there are various ways of achieving it as shown in Fig. 8.3.

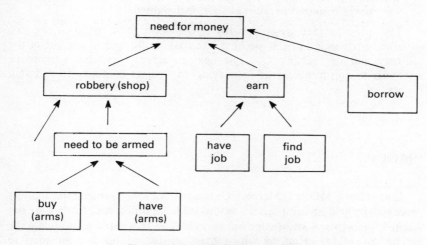

Figure 8.3   Plan of action in PAM

One of these is ROB < SHOP > where the category < SHOP > can include banks. One needs to be armed in order to rob a shop (or bank), which explains the taking of a gun and the answer to the first question.

The answering of the other two questions involves the script ROBBING A SHOP, in which there are characters of two types, the robbers and the robbed. Their respective actions are explained by a range of motivations, the robbers wanting money and not wanting to be caught, the robbed not wanting to be wounded, and so on. These models are both simply structured and simple-minded, and being usually ad hoc cannot be generalized to any significant extent.

Limitations of scripts

Since scripts have been conceived as fragments of stereotyped knowledge it is difficult to arrange for processes or items of information that are common to a number of scripts to be shared if these scripts do not form a hierarchy, where each may for example represent a specialization of the one above. The RESTAURANT script for example, has a part MEAL in common with EATING AT HOME. But it would be difficult to generalize "customer refuses to pay because steak is overcooked" to "general refusal to pay because of bad service" which could arise also in the GARAGE script.[9]

Roger Schank tells the following story:[10]

> I am always complaining because my wife never serves the meat as rare as I should like. One day when I was complaining about this to Bob Abelson he said, "That reminds me of how once when I was in England I wanted my hair cut very short—that was the style in America at the time—and they never managed to cut it as short as I wanted."

The question that arises is, what is the point in common in the two situations? It seems to be something like "asking for something out of the ordinary and not getting it". The next paragraph describes a tentative approach to this problem of identifying the points common to different scripts.

"MOPs"

Like scripts, MOPs[11] (Memory Organization Packets) enable the analysis process to be held up until certain conditions hold; unlike scripts, they are not isolated fragments of knowledge but include links that explain and relate the various knowledge items of which they consist. MOPs are intended to represent such general human characteristics as the wish to be right, to be happy, to get the better of a conflict, which can explain at a relatively high level of abstraction many of our styles of behavior.

The MOP scheme of knowledge organization is used in two programs in particular: BORIS[12] attempts to achieve an understanding at some depth of the motives of people involved in divorce cases; CYRUS[13] represents various episodes in the life of the diplomat Cyrus Vance.

CYRUS was developed to test an hypothesis formulated by several psychologists, mainly Bartlett,[14] concerning the reconstructive mechanisms that are implied in the processes of memorization and recall. The value of attempting to construct such a program is that it forces us to provide all the details, and to analyze in depth all the mental processes we believe are involved in recalling events, when we are not sure of the psychological basis for these processes.

The originality of CYRUS is mainly in the way its memory is organized. The events represented by the MOPs are organized in three different ways:

— hierarchically
— by causal, temporal and other relations between defining characteristics
— by the same relations between indices.

The revival of automatic translation

The lack of success in automatic translation in the 1950 – 1960 decade was attributed to the lack of "understanding" in the programs that were developed for this task; these programs simply manipulated the words of the language in the way they would handle any other symbols, taking no account of the fact that language is a tool for communication between humans which enables ideas to be exchanged. Today the problem is being attacked along two main lines. In the first, the input text is converted into a tree structure representing the syntactic structure of each phrase, possibly augmented by semantic information taken from a dictionary; this is then manipulated by a transfer grammar[15,16] to produce syntactically correct phrases in the output language. The second method takes much less account of syntax but uses a much more detailed conceptual representation of the sentences, involving a deep understanding of the text to be translated. This second approach has been used by Yorick Wilks[17] and Schank's group, several examples of whose work are described below.

The SAM program exploits the possibilities of scripts and of the Conceptual Dependency representation of sentences to derive the meaning of input sentences in several languages, notably Russian and Spanish, and thus indicates several possibilities for automatic translation.[18] The method consists of

(1) an analysis of the sentences input in the source language, leading to a Conceptual Dependency schema;
(2) generation of the output text in the object language, using discriminatory networks whenever a word having several meanings is encountered in the internal representation.

We shall concentrate on the second process here; notice that this method, which uses an internal language that is independent of the input language, requires only $2n$ programs for translation between n natural languages, instead of the $n(n-1)$ required by transfer methods which deal with the languages in pairs.

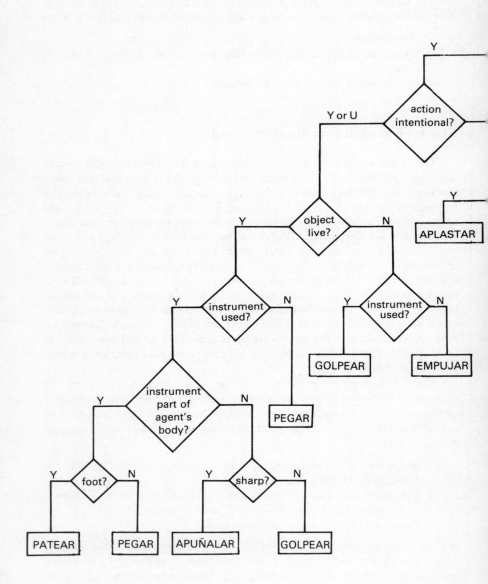

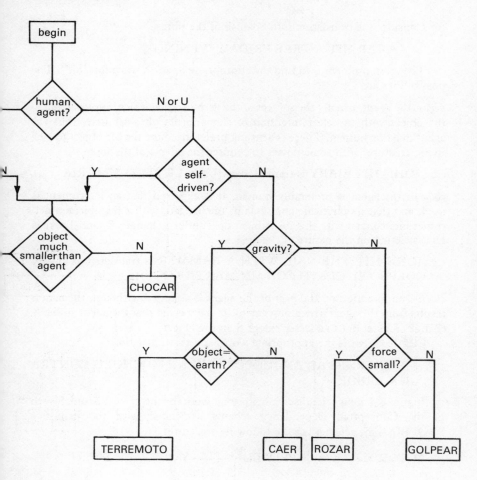

**Figure 8.4   Use of conceptual dependence representation to decide correct
Spanish translation of English verb TO HIT.** (Y = YES, N = NO, U = UNKNOWN)

Consider the translation into Spanish of the phrase

A CAR HIT A TREE FRIDAY EVENING

The main problem is to find the appropriate Spanish word for "hit". The possibilities are:

pegar: the agent, usually the subject of the verb in active voice, applies force to the object with the clear intention of changing its physical state; thus the agent must be human. There is a strong preference here for the object to be a living creature, with some power to counter the effects of the force.

e.g., JOHN HIT MARY is translated as JUAN LE PEGO A MARIA

golpear: the agent is preferably human. It is expected that an instrument is used, and that its physical state remains unchanged, whilst the object which comes into contact with this instrument does suffer a change of state. There is no restriction on the nature of the object.

e.g. JOHN HIT THE NAIL WITH A HAMMER is translated as JUAN GOLPEO EL CLAVO CON UN MARTILLO

chocar: no intention on the part of the agent is assumed, although the action results from the agent's own movement. It is expected that the agent suffers a change of state, but to a lesser extent than the object.

Clearly *chocar* is the appropriate word, and the translation is

EL VIERNES AL ANOCHECER UN AUTO CHOCO CONTRA UN ARBOL

Figure 8.4 shows the discriminatory network for the correct Spanish verb in the Conceptual Dependency schema associated with the primitive PROPEL. This schema has the following structure:

$$\text{ACTOR X} < == > \text{PROPEL} < \xrightarrow{\text{object}} Y < \xrightarrow{\text{instrument}} Z$$

Notes and references

[1] Rumelhart D. (1975), "Notes on a schema for stories", in *Representation and understanding*, D. Bobrow & A. Collins (eds.).
[2] Propp V. (1970), *Morphologie du conte*, (French translation), Paris, Seuil.
[3] Schank R. C., Abelson R. (1977), *Scripts, plans, goals and understanding*, Lawrence Erlbaum Assoc., Hillsdale, N.J.
[4] Cullingford R. E. (1978), *Script application: Computer understanding of newspaper stories*, Yale University.
[5] Bonnet A. (1979), "Schema-shift strategies for understanding texts in Natural Language", *Stanford University Technical Report* HPP-25.

6 Bonnet A. (1980), "Analyse de textes au moyen d'une grammaire sémantique et de schémas. Application à la compréhension de résumés médicaux en langage naturel", *Thèse d'État,* Université Paris VI.

7 Sabah G. (1980), "Contribution à la compréhension effective d'un récit", *Thèse d'Etat,* Université Paris VI.

8 Wilensky R. (1978), "Understanding goal-based stories", *Research Report 140,* Department of Computer Science, Yale University.

9 Dyer M. G. (1981), "$Restaurant revisited or lunch with Boris", *IJCAI-81,* Vancouver, Canada.

10 "A conversation with Roger Schank", in *Psychology today,* April 1983, pp. 28-36.

11 Schank R. C. (1981), "Reminding and memory organization, an introduction to MOPs", in *Strategies for Natural Language Processing,* W. Lehnert & M. Ringle (eds.), Lawrence Erlbaum, Hillsdale, N.J.

12 Lehnert W., Dyer M. G., Johnson P. N., Yang C. J., Harley S. (1983), "BORIS an experiment in in-depth understanding of narratives", *Artificial Intelligence,* vol. 20, 1.

13 Kolodner J. L. (1982), "Reconstructive Memory: A Computer Model", *Cognitive Science.*

14 Bartlett F. (1932), *Remembering: A study in experimental and social psychology,* London, Cambridge University Press.

15 Kittredge R., Bourbeau L., Isabelle P. (1976), "Design and implementation of an English-French transfer grammar", *Coling-76, Ottawa, Canada.*

16 Boitet C. (1976), "Problèmes actuels en T.A.: Un essai de réponse", *Coling-76,* Ottawa, Canada.

17 Wilks Y. (1973), "An artificial intelligence approach to machine translation", in *Computer Models of Thought and Language,* Schank and Colby (eds.), pp. 114-151, Freeman, San Francisco.

18 Carbonell J., Cullingford R. E., Gershman A. V. (1978), *Knowledge-based machine translation,* University of Yale, Department of Computer Science, Research Report 146.

Part Three

Representation of Knowledge and of Reasoning Processes

INTRODUCTION

Representing knowledge in a computer consists of setting up a correspondence between a symbolic reasoning system and the outside world. The phrase "Robert went to Paris" could be represented in exactly that form, that is, by that particular string of characters; but then a query-and-response program would not be able to answer the question, "Who went to Paris?" because there is nothing in this string to help understanding of the phrase, in particular nothing to identify the agent of the action. A better representation, from this point of view, and one which comes to mind naturally, would be:

Action:	GO
Agent:	ROBERT
Source:	?
Destination:	PARIS
Tense:	PAST
Means:	?

This includes information that indicates the meaning of the phrase; but it still leaves much to be inferred, and which would be inferred by any human who heard the phrase. If we include this the representation becomes:

Action	GO	(type)	MOVEMENT
Agent	ROBERT	(type)	HUMAN BEING
Source	?	(default)	ROBERT'S HOME TOWN
Destination	PARIS	(type)	TOWN
		(equivalent)	CAPITAL OF FRANCE
Means:	?	(travel by)	TRAIN, AEROPLANE, CAR, . . .

Not all these inferences will necessarily be correct; however, any good system for representing knowledge must make it possible for inferential processes to be brought into play.

Just as no-one has yet succeeded in designing a universal programming language, no-one has yet produced an ideal form for representing knowledge in an AI system. Some forms are better than others for representing purely logical reasoning processes, others have advantages when it is a question of reasoning by analogy; and so on.

There is a classical philosophical distinction between "knowing what" and "knowing how"; the equivalent in AI is the distinction between "declarative knowledge" and "procedural knowledge". Knowledge items of the first type have the advantages of being easy to read and to modify, and of not requiring anything to be said in advance of how they are to be used. The disadvantage however, is that processing such knowledge items can take a relatively long time. Items of the second type, procedural items, have precisely the opposite advantages and disadvantages. Declarative items play the role of data in the procedures that interpret them and consequently are usually said to form a data structure. We have already had an example of the distinction between declarative and procedural knowledge in the case of analysis of natural language, between a grammar and the process of interpretation of the grammar. A data structure is not in itself "knowledge"; analogously, a book is only a source of knowledge and it is the combination of this source with an ability to read and to understand that produces knowledge.

Declarative structures are made use of by means of interpretive procedures; individual items can be used in different ways: for example, the rule $A \& B \rightarrow C$ can be used in any of the four following ways:

(1) if A and B are both true, then C is true
(2) if the aim is to prove the truth of C, then a possible method is to try to prove that both A and B are true
(3) if A is true and C is false, then B is false
(4) if C is false, then at least one of A, B is false.

We have a stock of factual knowledge about the world around us, such as "elephants have trunks", "dogs are animals"; we want, in AI, to be able to describe the properties of objects from their names and to find ways of classifying these objects. We want also to find ways of representing events, such as "Giscard met Brezhnev in Warsaw", "John killed Mary in anger".

The power of a method of representation can be judged by its ability to express complex situations precisely—see page 101 for the analysis of a complex statement—and also by its ability to represent the fact that two statements have something in common: thus in a geological information system "compacted limestone" and "porous limestone" should be represented as two particular forms of "limestone" and not as two unrelated substances. This second characteristic not only improves the clarity of the representation but also reduces the demands on memory because items having properties in common need be recorded only once, in the most general form, instead of as separate entries.

The power can be judged also by the ability to deal with imprecise arguments, especially inductive processes; the latter are always more difficult to represent than purely deductive processes. This brings in the idea of "commonsense" reasoning, which differs from formal logic and mathematics in that it is used when a decision has to be based on incomplete information.

In mathematics a conclusion is not accepted as valid unless it can be reached by applying the accepted logical rules to the initial axioms; but in real life we often have to face the fact that our knowledge is limited and to draw conclusions for which we cannot give a rigorous proof but which seem to us plausible, often expressed as "reasonable". In this section the formalism of traditional logic will be described first, and then the emphasis placed on the need to be able to simulate this looser form of reasoning.

9
First-order Logic

This chapter deals with the formal logical system with which philosophers and mathematicians have been concerned for a long time. The idea of using this to represent reasoning and decision-making processes was first suggested in a paper by John McCarthy[1] in 1958. We describe first the propositional calculus, which is a useful tool but which is unable to express the majority of the problems with which AI deals, and then its extension to the predicate calculus, giving several examples of problems that can be expressed very readily in this latter formalism.

The propositional calculus

This is defined by two sets of rules: those of the syntax, governing the form of the statements that can be made in the language, and those governing the derivation of new statements from old.

To every legal statement, called a proposition, one of two possible values TRUE and FALSE is assigned; these are often called Boolean values, after the mathematician and logician George Boole (1815–1864). For example, "Reagan is the President of the USA", "Madrid is the capital of Belgium"—only one of which is TRUE at this moment (1984). More complex propositions can be expressed by using logical *connectives*, usually written as follows:

AND	∧	or	&
OR (inclusive)	∨		
NOT	⌐	or	~
IMPLIES	⇒	or	⊃
EQUIVALENT	≡		

With these, propositions such as "the socks are either on the table or in the drawer", or "Henry is neither a mathematician nor a physicist" can be expressed in formal language: notice that OR is inclusive in this language, whilst in everyday life it is more often exclusive—as in the statement about the socks. Formally, the proposition A ∨ B is TRUE if either A or B is TRUE, and also if both are TRUE, but if the truth of either A or B has been established there is no need to consider this second possibility.

The proposition "A ≡ B" is TRUE if A and B are either both TRUE or both FALSE, and FALSE if A and B have different values.

"A ⇒ B" means that if A is TRUE then so is B; thus the statement A ⇒ B is TRUE if B is TRUE and equally if A is FALSE. This last assertion may seem surprising, but its validity is shown by an example such as "If I am in Paris then I am in France", which is equivalent to "Either I am in France or I am not in Paris". The truth value of an implication is not always intuitively obvious: thus "If horses can talk then pigs can fly" is TRUE. "¬ A" is TRUE if A is FALSE, and conversely.

The following table effectively defines the five connectives.

A	B	A ∧ B	A ∨ B	A ⇒ B	¬ A	A ≡ B
T	T	T	T	T	F	T
T	F	F	T	F	F	F
F	T	F	T	T	T	F
F	F	F	F	T	T	T

The propositional calculus is based on the rule called *modus ponens,* which states that if P ⇒ Q and P is TRUE then Q is TRUE also. This is written formally

$$(A \wedge (A \Rightarrow B)) \Rightarrow B$$

There are also two rules called de Morgan's Laws:

$$\neg (A \wedge B) \equiv \neg A \vee \neg B$$
$$\neg (A \vee B) \equiv \neg A \wedge \neg B$$

and the formal expression of the *reductio ab absurdum* method of reasoning:

$$(A \Rightarrow B) \equiv (\neg B \Rightarrow \neg A)$$

The application of this is that if the aim is to prove that A ⇒ B, this can be achieved by assuming that B is FALSE and showing that A is then FALSE, which contradicts the hypothesis that A is TRUE; B must therefore be TRUE.

The predicate calculus

The propositional calculus is unable to express many statements that are of interest in AI, and in other fields also; in particular, if we wish to state facts about objects in the real world we must be able to identify individual objects (the question of instantiation) and to say to what set of objects certain statements apply—for example, does a particular statement apply to all objects belonging to a certain class? The predicate calculus is an extension of the propositional calculus that allows us to do this, with the aid of the ideas of *predicates* and *quantifiers*, the latter being of two kinds, *existential* and *universal* respectively; the most important difference from the propositional calculus is the introduction of the concept of a *variable*.

A predicate is a function of one or more arguments, returning one or other of the values TRUE, FALSE; thus the predicate DOG defined by

DOG(X): "X is a DOG"

takes the value TRUE if X = ROVER and FALSE if X = PUSSY.

It is conventional to use the last letters of the alphabet (e.g., X, Y, Z) for variables and the first (e.g., A, B, C) or symbolic identifiers such as PUSSY or MADRID for constants. A predicate can define a relation or specify an action: thus the predicate

GIVES (X, Y, Z)

can mean "X GIVES Y to Z".

A *function* is a generalization of the concept of predicate, able to return a value of any type, Boolean, symbolic or numerical; thus the function

CAPITAL (X)

returns the value ROME when X = ITALY.

Functions and predicates can be combined, but not without restrictions. For example, the predicate DOG and the function CAPITAL, as just defined, can be combined in the order DOG (CAPITAL (X)), because if, say X = ENGLAND, the predicate to be evaluated is DOG (LONDON), which presumably has the value FALSE. The inverse order CAPITAL (DOG (X)), however, leads to the function CAPITAL (FALSE)—meaning "what is the capital city of FALSE?"—which is clearly a nonsensical question.

Quantifiers

As just said, there are two of these: the universal quantifier $\forall$, meaning "for all . . ." and the existential quantifier $\exists$, meaning "there is . . .".

Example: "every dog is an animal" is expressed as
($\forall$ X) (DOG (X) $\Rightarrow$ ANIMAL (X))
"every boy has a bicycle" is expressed as
($\forall$ X) ($\exists$Y) (BOY (X) $\Rightarrow$ BICYCLE (Y) $\land$ OWN (X, Y))

the second statement meaning that whoever is the boy X, there is a bicycle Y such that Y is owned by X.

Rules of inference

The rules of the system enable new statements to be derived from those already existing, using the two principles of *modus ponens,* defined above, and *universal specialization* respectively; the second consists in replacing a quantified variable by a constant:

$$(\forall \, x) \, (P \, (x)) \; \Rightarrow \; P(A)$$

The general process is called substitution, and the particular case of making two quantified expressions identical by means of appropriate substitutions is called unification. The unification algorithm conceived by Robinson[2] has had an important influence on research in theorem proving: see, for example, Nilsson.[3]

Application to solving a problem: stacking blocks

Figure 9.1 shows a problem to be solved. A, B, C are three identical blocks, initially arranged as on the left with A and B resting on the table and C

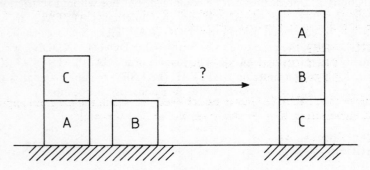

Figure 9.1   The problem to be solved

resting on A; B is FREE, meaning that no block is resting on B. The problem is to change the arrangement to that on the right, where C rests on the table, B on C and A on B; with the rule that only one block may be moved at a time.
The initial configuration can be expressed thus:

IC: ON (C, A)
ONTABLE (A)
ONTABLE (B)
FREE (C)
FREE (B)

and the final configuration, the goal, is

FC: ON (A, B)
ON (B, C)
ONTABLE (C)

The predicate FREE has to be defined, and rules given saying how a block can be made free. The program is given the following, which it tries to apply in various orders.

1. FREE (X) $\Rightarrow$ $\neg$ ($\exists$ y) ON (y, x)
meaning that if a block is free, there is no other block resting on it.
2. ON (Y, X) $\wedge$ REMOVE (Y, X) $\Rightarrow$ FREE (X) $\wedge$ $\neg$ ON (Y, X)
defining the action REMOVE so as to free a block not already free.
3. FREE (X) $\wedge$ FREE (Y) $\wedge$ STACK (X, Y) $\Rightarrow$ ON (X, Y)
defining the action STACK, resulting in one block resting on another.

Armed with these rules, the program has to find a sequence of actions that will change the configuration from the initial IC to the final FC; the problem is an example of *productions*, discussed in Chapter 12.

The strategy is to try to achieve a sequence of sub-goals. Taking ON (A, B) as the first, the program looks to see if there are any rules leading to ON (X, Y): Rule 3 is such, so the program tries to apply this, substituting X = A, Y = B and giving as the first sub-goal:

SG1:   FREE (A)
FREE (B) (already satisfied)
STACK (A, B)

To achieve this, FREE (A) has to be achieved, for which the program applies Rule 2, substituting X = A; this gives the second sub-goal

SG2:   ON (Y, A)
REMOVE (Y, A)

ON (Y, A) is easily achieved by substituting Y = C, since ON (C, A) is given initially. This gives REMOVE (C, A) as the first real action to be performed. The condition FREE (A) of SB1 now holds, so the second action STACK (A, B) is now possible.

To achieve the final goal, ON (B, C) has to be achieved; this can be done by applying Rule 3, implying a further sub-goal:

SG3:   FREE (B)
       FREE (C)
       STACK (B, C)

By Rule 1, FREE (B) $\Rightarrow$ ($\forall$y) $\urcorner$ ON (y, B) $\Rightarrow$ $\urcorner$ ON (A, B)
(i.e. if B is free, there is no block resting on B and therefore A cannot be resting on B); so by Rule 2 the action REMOVE (A, B) must be performed, destroying the result of the previous action STACK (A, B): the system has no means of telling, from the rules as given, that REMOVE is the inverse action to STACK. But once ON (B, C) has been achieved, as above, the further action STACK (A, B) solves the problem.

This example shows that an appropriate ordering of the sub-goals can give a quicker solution to a problem. Here, the sub-goals ON (A, B) and ON (B, C) are not independent; achieving the first hinders the achieving of the second, whilst the second is of no hindrance to the first. If this constraint had been studied at the start, the unnecessary action ON (A, B), which resulted in a check and a need for back-tracking, would have been avoided. It is the use of this "heuristic" type of reasoning—observing that achieving one sub-goal may block the achieving of another—that differentiates a search guided by high-level rules from a blind search. The plan-generating program NOAH of Earl Sacerdoti[4] gives very good results with problems needing this type of attack.

Many problems of an essentially deductive nature, such as the one just discussed or the famous Tower of Hanoi problem,* can be expressed very well in terms of first-order logic; but these are really just logical games and the majority of problems that humans are faced with are of a much more inductive nature. An example is the interpretation of a patient's medical record. Such problems require the handling of data that are uncertain and may even be wrong; a solution is reached only by complex reasoning processes, such as putting forward a tentative hypothesis to be confirmed gradually as other information becomes available, making many cross-checks to detect errors, and so on. It is for this reason that formalisms other than that of first-order logic have been developed to enable the nature of human reasoning to be taken into account.

First-order logic was the first technique to be used for querying a database, for example in SIR.[5] Green[6] has given an example in which a clause containing free variables is associated with a query and the program has to find the items in the database to which these are to be tied, in order to answer

---

* In the problem of the Tower of Hanoi there are three pegs fixed to a baseboard and on one peg are a number N of disks all of different radii, stacked in increasing order of size from the smallest at the top to the largest at the bottom, resting on the board. The problem is to transfer the stack from the present peg to one of the other with the rules that only one disk may be moved at a time and no disk may ever rest on a smaller one; the third peg may be used as necessary in the process. There is a discussion of this problem in the context of predicate calculus in Nilsson.[3]

the question; and the use of logic in databases is discussed in Gallaire and Minker's book.[7] Levesque[8] on the other hand, has taken a particular interest in databases in which the information is incomplete. For example, if the question is "How many children has Mary?" a program that assumes that the information is complete will simply count the number of individuals satisfying the criterion "is a child of Mary". Levesque contends that in order to answer such a question correctly there must be a language available in which both the domain of the question and what the database knows about this domain can be described.

Notes and references

[1] McCarthy J. (1968), "Programs with common sense", in *Semantic information processing*, M. Minsky (ed.), Cambridge, Mass. MIT Press. (Article originally appeared in 1958).

[2] Robinson J. A. (1965), "A machine-oriented logic based on the resolution principle", *JACM 12* (1), pp. 23-41.

[3] Nilsson N. (1980), *Principles of Artificial Intelligence*, Palo Alto, California, Tioga Publishing Company.

[4] Sacerdoti E.D. (1975), "A structure for plans and behavior", *Technical Note 109*, AI Center, SRI International, Menlo Park, California.

[5] Raphael B. (1968), "SIR: A computer program for semantic information retrieval", in *Semantic information processing*, Cambridge, Mass., MIT Press (original article in 1964).

[6] Green C. (1969), "The application of theorem-proving to question-answering systems", *Ph.D. thesis*, Dept of Electrical Engineering, Stanford University.

[7] Gallaire H., Minker J. (eds.) (1978), *Logic and databases*, New York, Plenum Press.

[8] Levesque H. J. (1983), "The logic of incomplete knowledge bases", in *Conceptual Modelling: perspectives from artificial intelligence, Databases and programming languages*, Brodie, Mylopoulos and Schmidt (eds.), New York, Springer-Verlag.

10

Procedural
Representation

Introduction

There is nothing in a declarative knowledge item to say how it should be used; a procedural item, in contrast, contains within itself explicit information on this point. The former has the nature of an item of data to be used by a program, whilst the latter is the program itself; it follows from the definition—a statement that may seem tautological—that procedural representation is the only one of the five types described in this section of the book for which the advantage of as great as possible use of the declarative form is not emphasized.

The difference between declarative and procedural representation is well illustrated by the example of analysis of natural language. A noun clause can be given as a declarative statement in terms of a few rules of a grammar; these rules are executed by a program able to decide whether or not the sequence of words forming the phrase to be analyzed does or does not satisfy a number of grammatical criteria; if in this process one rule fails to give a decision, another can be tried. A procedural representation includes the program that scans the words and the rule that defines the noun clause. The observant reader will not fail to notice that a declarative item cannot stand alone but must be complemented by an interpreting procedure; thus a system cannot be entirely declarative, but it can be entirely procedural. A highly declarative system will be written in a language having a very wide syntax and therefore allowing a great variety of information to be expressed in this form; a limited syntax forces the programmer to relegate most of the information to the procedural parts.

As an example, consider the representation of the phrase

all Ruritanian and Moribundian soldiers are rogues

The declarative form, using the language of first-order logic, is

(∀x) (soldier (x) ∧ (Ruritanian (x) ∨ Moribundian (x))) ⇒ rogue (x)

The procedural form, using the language MICRO-PLANNER,[1] is

(CONSEQUENT (ROGUE?x)
   (GOAL (SOLDIER?x)
     (OR (GOAL RURITANIAN?x))
     (GOAL (MORIBUNDIAN?x))))

The declarative statement can be used to decide whether or not a given person is a rogue, and also to prove that a soldier who is not a rogue is not a Ruritanian. The procedural form can be used in this way: to prove that an individual X is a rogue, prove first that he is a soldier; if that succeeds, prove next that he is a Ruritanian—if this succeeds, this completes the proof; if it fails, prove that he is a Moribundian. The order of the terms in the expression is important and the direction in which the inferences are made is quite specific.

We now consider the relative advantages and disadvantages of the two forms; this was the subject of a famous controversy[2] in the early 1970s.

Advantages of declarative forms

Readability. Statements of data—using the term in its widest sense—are much easier to read than programs, especially by non-specialists; the relevance of this general principle here is shown by the example just given.

Economy and flexibility. A statement involving several variables needs only be written once in declarative form, and can be used in different ways on different occasions according to the results sought; but a procedural form must be repeated in every procedure that uses it, because the direction of the inference and the constraints on the variables may vary from one to the next. Thus the declarative form has the advantages of economy and flexibility.

Ease of modification. A declarative structure is easier to modify and new statements can be added more easily. This is particularly important for the evolution of the system and for giving it an ability to learn from experience, that is, to modify itself: see Chapter 19.

Advantages of procedural forms

Meta-knowledge. Some items of "second level" knowledge—a kind of meta- knowledge—are most easily expressed in procedural form: for example, the relation "is near to" can be treated as transitive provided it is not used too many times in a single deductive chain. The declarative form does not suit such information well, because its use requires access to the deep structure of the computation, in recursive procedures for example.

Dependence of form on future use. In theory, statements can often be written without regard for the use that will be made of them later in the program; but in practice the programmer will always have this in mind. Consider this type of statement, used for diagnosing plant diseases:

If there are spots on the leaves, and if the spots are cankered, it is likely that such-and-such a fungus is present.

Clearly, the second ("and if . . .") clause is to be evaluated only if the first is TRUE; whoever wrote the program knew that the interpreting procedure would evaluate the clauses in a statement in a certain order, usually the order in which they were written.

Ultimate necessity. There is always a final level at which any declarative statement has to be interpreted and executed by some procedure; put otherwise, there is always an irreducible kernel that must be programmed and must therefore be of procedural form.

General assessment of procedural systems

Procedural languages are typified by MICRO-PLANNER; a knowledge base consists of statements and "theorems", the latter being processes that are activated whenever the base is modified and whenever an appropriate precondition is satisfied.

Apart from the fact that in these procedures the inferences are always made in explicitly specified directions, the main difference from productions—see Chapter 12—is that the theorems can call each other, whilst production rules never intercommunicate directly but only via an interpreter. This property gives production systems the advantage of modularity and in consequence has caused the use of pure procedural systems to be largely abandoned. A further disadvantage is the difficulty of controlling the number of inferences made by a procedural system, which has been seen by many researchers as an argument against their use in large-scale applications.

Notes and references

[1] Hewitt C. (1972), "Description and theoretical analysis (using schemata) of PLANNER: a language for proving theorems and manipulating models in a robot". *Memo AI-TR-258*, MIT.

[2] Winograd T. (1975), "Frame representations and the declarative/procedural controversy", in *Representation and understanding: studies in cognitive science*, Bobrow and Collins (eds.), New York, Academic Press, pp. 185-210.

11
Semantic Networks

Introduction

A semantic network is a set of points called *nodes* joined by *arcs;* in general, the nodes represent concepts and the arcs give the relations between these. Simple nodes are named with the name of the concept, more complex nodes do not necessarily have names and are themselves semantic sub-networks. The idea of using semantic networks to represent human knowledge is usually attributed to Quillian.[1]

The phrase "Rover chases Tabby" can be represented by:

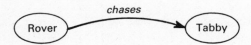

or non-graphically by, for example (CHASE ROVER TABBY).

A concept is usually linked to a group or family of which it is a member; denoting "is an element of" by "e" a slightly more complex network can be given:

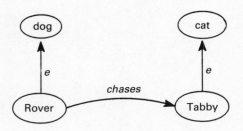

96

Evolution of the network representation

A slightly more complex phrase is "Rover chases the cat with long fur". This states that "Rover (a dog) chases an individual that is a cat that possesses something (fur) that has property of being long" and can be represented as follows, where "p" denotes "possesses":

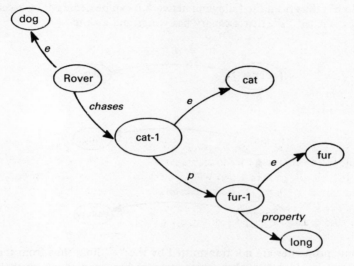

Unlabelled nodes are usually particular instances of more general concepts, and if necessary can be labelled with a suffixed name, as in "cat-1" above; they are linked to the parent concept by an arc labelled "e" to denote the relation. The "e" relation links an individual to a group or family of which it is a member; a further relation, which we denote by "s", "is a sub-set of", relates the group to a larger, more general class. Thus "Rover is a dog which is an animal" can be expressed:

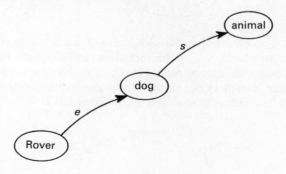

Notice that the node "Rover" could be labelled "Rover-1" to indicate that this particular dog was a member of the family of dogs named Rover, and joined by an "e" arc to a node "Rover". Notice also that in the phrase "Rover is a dog which is an animal" the two instances of "is" have different meanings, and must be treated differently by any reasoning mechanisms applied to the network.

Properties possessed by parent concepts are often "inherited" by their "children"; thus from the following network it can be deduced, by ascending the arcs labelled "s", that a canary has wings and a skin:

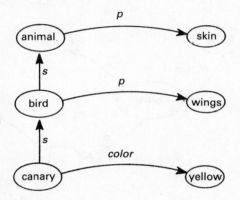

Some properties are not transmitted by the "e" link; thus from the next diagram we could deduce that robins in general are studied by ornithologists but could not say with certainty that the particular robin Paul is:

William Woods[2] and Gary Hendrix[3] have drawn attention to the dangers of the lack of standardization in this formalism, and especially to the need for rules concerning what may be represented by the arcs so as to reduce the risk of making false inferences as a result of following a chain of links.

The problem with even so simple a representation as:

is that if we want to add "with a hammer" we do not know where to put this; and this leads to the idea of representing the action "strike" as the central element. With this, the phrase "John struck Mary with a hammer in the park last night" can be represented by the following diagram.

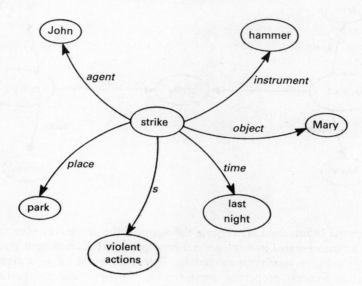

Such a representation, however, is inadequate for a phrase of the type "John struck Mary and Henry punched James". If this is shown as follows, it is not clear who struck whom:

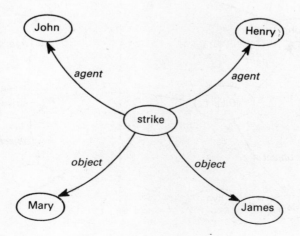

It is better therefore to represent two occurrences of the same action, here given the general name of STRIKE, as follows:

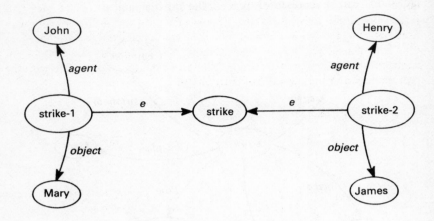

General information concerning the agent of the action, the object, etc. could be incorporated into the general concept STRIKE, making it possible to apply tests for validity to the phrase. This is shown in the next diagram, where the general properties are given on the right and the particular occurrence on the left:

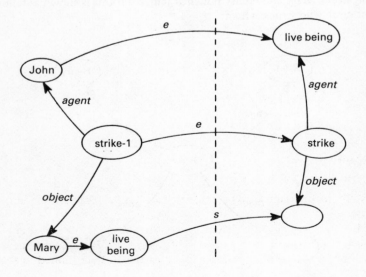

Notice that we have gone from a form in which the concept STRIKE is represented by an arc to one in which it appears as a node; it has become a predicate with a number of more or less standard arguments such as agent and object, and also, if necessary, others such as instrument, time, place, etc. This is similar to Fillmore's case grammar,[4] apart from the detail that he represents time not as a case but as a mode. The diagram below expresses the fact that "the dog guarded the house carefully all day"; Simmons[5] has made important contributions to the understanding of natural language in connection with the representation of the meaning of such phrases.

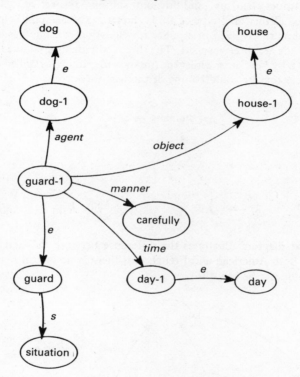

Taxonomies

Many natural and experimental sciences have extensive taxonomies that can be simply represented by tree structures in which the nodes are the relevant concepts and the arcs indicate relations such as "is a subset of" or "is an element of". These trees can be regarded as simplified semantic networks; they are in fact semantic networks in which the arcs are limited to showing hierarchical relations such as those just referred to; these relations are used by the processes that manipulate the network as mechanisms governing inheritance, that is, for transmitting properties from an ancestor node (representing a general property) to its descendants (representing more specialized properties).

The "e" and "s" types of arc already introduced do not always suffice to specify the relation between sibling nodes, that is, between nodes having a common parent; more specialized types are therefore introduced in certain formalisms, particularly in partitioned semantic networks:[3] "de" and "ds", meaning "distinct elements" and "disjoint subsets" respectively.

The value of the "de" type of arc is shown in the diagram below. Peter, Paul and John are involved in a police investigation: a crime has been committed and they are three suspects. The three individuals are linked to the set of HUMANS by "de" arcs whilst the (unknown) criminal is linked by an "e" arc to indicate that he could be one of the first three.

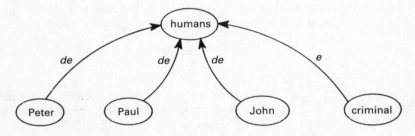

The next diagram illustrates the difference between "s" and "ds". No city can be both American and French, but there is no logical reason why a big city should not be beautiful.

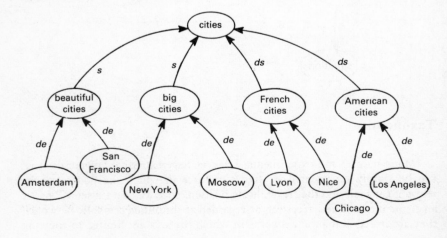

The use of these further types of arc increases the power of the network; thus in this example a processing program can deduce that Lyon is not an American city, but there is nothing to prevent the program from deciding that Amsterdam is a big city.

Partitioning semantic networks

The idea of the partitioned semantic network, introduced by Gary Hendrix,[3] enables sets of nodes and arcs to be grouped together in abstract spaces defining the scope of the various relations. Each node and each arc belongs to one or more of these spaces; there can be links between nodes in different spaces but all such links must be regarded as crossing the boundaries of the spaces. The spaces define the partitioning of the network.

The diagram below, after Hendrix, gives the representation of the phrase "There is a man who has a car". This illustrates an important property of partitioned networks, that the existential quantifier is implied when a structure is assigned to a space. Here the space S1 contains background information, for example on people and the possession of cars, that could be of help in understanding the statement. S2 represents "a certain man M" whose syntactic role in the statement is the subject. S3 represents a particular instance of possession P and is the translation, into this form, of the fragment "has a car".

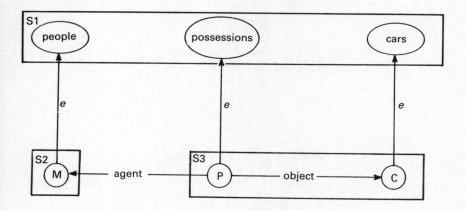

A second example is the partitioning for "Paul drinks wine or Mary eats cheese":

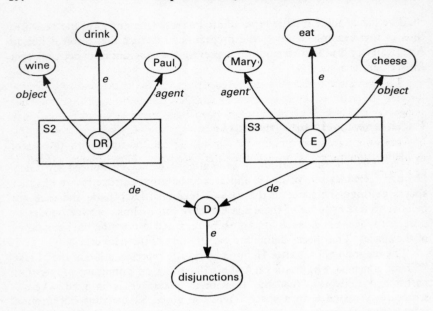

Logical negation is represented analogously to disjunction, the node D being replaced by "N" and "DISJUNCTIONS" by "NEGATIONS". Implication can be represented either by using the logical equivalence:

$$(A ==> B) \equiv (B \lor \neg A)$$

or directly as shown in this diagram;

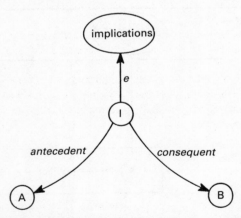

Implication has the attraction of representing the universal quantifier; again following Hendrix[3] we can write:

$$(\forall x \in X) \, p(x) <=> (\nabla x) \, (member \, (x, X) ==> P(x))$$

the force of which is that any universally quantified formula can be translated into an implication.

There is no special representation for logical conjugation, because this is implicit.

The semantic network representations given as examples are effective only to the extent that programs are available that can handle them. Such programs will operate as unification algorithms, meaning that they will seek to replace the variables, which are unknown quantities whose value is sought, by constants; and will do this by comparing the question with the set of available statements. For example, the question "Who drinks wine?" is represented:

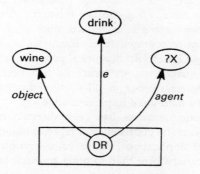

Using pattern matching techniques to compare this with the diagram for "Paul drinks wine" given previously, a program can easily find the solution "X = PAUL". The process is exactly equivalent to that given in Chapter 9, on first-order logic.

It often happens that the answer to a question cannot be given directly but requires some traversing of the network in order to use relations or attributes concerning implied entities. Schubert[6] has introduced what he calls an "access skeleton" for this purpose; the following example shows that if the question is "Is Jumbo an elephant?" we may have to examine the colour, texture, shape, etc. of the object in question to find if these particular values could characterize an elephant.

```
             :  specialization/
             :  generalization
elephant --  :                      :  size, shape
             :                                         :  color
             :  physical qualities --  :
             :                         :  external    :  appearance --  :
                                       :  qualities--                   :  texture
```

Conclusion

Semantic networks have been used in the construction of expert systems, among which PROSPECTOR, concerned with mineral prospecting (see Chapter 17), has made the greatest use of the technique. This chapter has attempted to show how the power of a network increases with the complexity of the formalism. There must always be a compromise between the complexity of a data structure and that of the interpreting program; the better the structure is indexed, the better the interpreter is guided. The study of the structuring of semantic networks has led to the increasing use of representations that are hybrids between production rules and structured objects, two subjects described in the two following chapters.

Attempts have been made to introduce more rigor and more standardization into this form of representation. Examples are: Ronald Brachman[7] author of the language KLONE;[8] Shapiro's[9] proposal to use first-order logic, mainly the logical quantifiers; the work of Schubert;[10] and Fahlman's[11] proposal for an architecture that would allow computations to be made in parallel by means of a hardwired implementation.

Work on semantic networks has been directed increasingly towards improving the precision and consistency of representation of concepts that are relevant to practical applications. More consideration has been given to philosophical implications here than in other research into representation of knowledge.

Notes and references

[1] Quillian M. R. (1968), "Semantic memory", in *Semantic Information Processing*, M. Minsky (ed.), Cambridge, Mass., MIT Press, pp. 227-270.

[2] Woods W. (1975), *What's in a link? Foundations for semantic networks*, *Representation and Understanding*, Bobrow and Collins (eds.), New York, Academic Press, pp. 35-82.

[3] Hendrix G. (1979), "Encoding knowledge in partitioned networks", in *Associative Networks*, N. Findler (ed.), New York, Academic Press, pp. 51-92.

[4] Fillmore C. (1968), "The case for case", in Bach and Harms (eds.), *Universals in Linguistic theory*, Chicago, Holt, Rinehart and Winston.

[5] Simmons R. F. (1973), "Semantic networks: their computation and use for understanding English sentences", in *Computer Models of Thought and Language*, Schank and Colby (eds.), Freeman, San Francisco.

[6] Schubert L. K., Goebel R. G., Cercone N. J. (1979), "Structure and organization of a semantic net", in *Associative networks*, Findler (ed.), New York, Academic Press, pp. 121-175.

[7] Brachman R. J. (1977), "What's in a concept: Structural foundations for semantic networks", *International Journal of Man-machine Studies*, 9, 2, pp. 127-152.

[8] Brachman R. J. (1979), "On the epistemological status of semantic networks", in *Associative networks: representation and use of knowledge by computers,* Findler (ed.), New York, Academic Press, pp. 3-50.

[9] Shapiro S. C. (1971), "A net structure for semantic information storage, deduction and retrieval", *Advance papers of IJCAI-71,* pp. 512-523.

[10] Schubert L. K. (1976), "Extending the expressive power of semantic networks", *Artificial Intelligence 7,* 2, pp. 163-198.

[11] Fahlman S. E. (1979), *NETL: a system for representing and using real-world knowledge,* Cambridge, Mass., MIT Press.

12
Production Rules

Introduction

The formalism of production rules had been used in several fields well before the advent of artificial intelligence; for example, in symbolic logic by Post[1] in certain algorithms conceived by Markov, and in linguistics by Chomsky,[2] in the last case in the form of rewrite rules* for syntactic recognition of phrases in natural language.

A production rule is a situation – action couple, meaning that whenever a certain situation is encountered, given as the left side of the rule, the action given on the right is performed; very often the action is the taking of some decision, but this need not always be the case. There is no a priori constraint on the form of the situation or of the action.

A system based on production rules will usually have three components:

(1) The rule base, consisting of the set of production rules.
(2) One or more data structures containing the known facts relevant to the domain of interest, possibly also some useful definitions; these are often called the facts bases.
(3) The interpreter of these facts and rules, which is the mechanism that decides which rule to apply and initiates the corresponding action.

The facts and the rules have a syntax that is known to the interpreter; the latter can therefore manipulate these logically, deciding on their truth or otherwise, in some programs deriving new facts from them or suppressing certain facts. There is not always a clear distinction between "data" and "facts": here we shall interpret "facts" to mean the permanent knowledge incorporated into the program, whilst the data relate to a particular problem.

---

*A rewrite rule states the equivalence of two sequences of symbols, e.g.,
<NOUN-GROUP> := <ARTICLE> <ADJECTIVE> <NOUN>

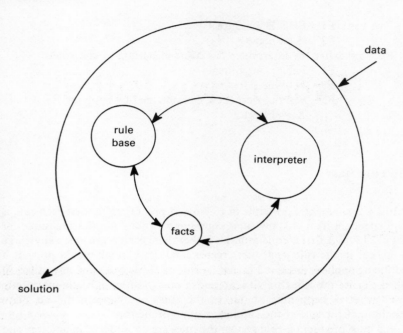

The conceptual separation of the production rules, expressed in as fully declarative a form as possible and therefore in as readable a form as possible, from the mechanism for interpretation, often called the inference engine, has not always been as clear as it is now. Many of the early production-rule systems were procedural programs containing both the knowledge base and the means for interpreting this knowledge. Even today there are systems containing rules that relate as much to the means for making inferences as they do to the inferences themselves. The clear separation of the two is a methodological advance that has had a profound influence on the concepts of AI and on the tools that have now been developed.

The simpler and more uniform the formalism of the production rules, the better the capacity of the system for learning, because the regularity favors both generalization and specialization of the existing rules. At the same time, a formalism that is too simple can limit the types of statement that can be represented in a particular domain. There is no ideal compromise in complexity between the formalism of the rules and that of the interpreter, as we have already mentioned in connection with representation by semantic networks.

Consider this simple example:

Rule base: R1   If X is an animal and X mews then X is a cat (one rule only)

Fact base: F1   Felix is an animal
F2   Felix mews
Fact base after the interpreter has scanned both facts and rules:
F1   Felix is an animal
F2   Felix mews
F3   Felix is a cat (new fact obtained by applying R1 with
X = Felix).

The rule base

It is a fundamental principle of rule-based programming that each rule is
an independent item of knowledge, containing all the conditions required for
its application. A first corollary of this is that there is no mechanism anywhere
else except in the rule itself that creates conditions which would prevent it
from being applied. A second is that no rule can ever call upon any other, so
that in a sense the rules are all ignorant of one another; only the interpreter
knows what is happening so far as the rules are concerned, and plays
something of the role of the conductor of an orchestra.

In a pure production-rule system the rules are not ordered in any way and
in principle any one can be activated at any moment; they are simply gathered
together without any knowledge of how they will be used. The order in which
they are in fact used is decided by the interpreter according to certain criteria,
some details of which are given in the section below on the resolution of
conflicts. There may of course be no strategy, the rules being used in the
order in which they are written.

The advantages of the production-rule method of representation can be
summarized as follows. Because of its considerable degree of modularity such
a system is easily modified, and so can evolve; the architectural structure is
not destroyed by the addition, deletion or modification of a rule; and there is
no need to take precautions against side-effects. In general, the more rules a
system has—assuming of course that they are sound—the more powerful and
the more detailed its conclusions will be.

Of course, it is not only the production-rule method that gives modular
systems; the use of structured objects, to be described in the next chapter, also
does this, but in a different way.

The main danger to be guarded against with systems that can evolve is the
loss of logical consistency, because beyond a certain size and if the number of
rules is large, say more than a few hundred, it becomes difficult to check by
hand whether or not a proposed new rule is redundant or even in conflict with
an existing rule. It is for this reason that sophisticated knowledge-gathering
systems have powerful mechanisms for helping the designer to avoid

introducing inconsistencies (see Chapter 14); such mechanisms include "friendly" interfaces and means for detecting similarities between rules.

Classification of interpreters

Forward or backward chaining?

One way of characterizing an interpreter (or "inference engine") is according to the way in which it tries to apply the rules, as a consequence of the facts that it studies. If it looks first at the established *data* or *facts* to decide if these satisfy the left side of a rule (the premise), it is said to work in the forward direction. If on the other hand it looks first at the *aims* to be attained as given on the right side of the rule (the action part) and then tries to satisfy only those rules which have these aims, it is said to work backwards. This distinction is precisely equivalent to that made in the case of interpreters for grammars, between *bottom-up*, equivalent to *forwards* because they start from the data, and *top-down*, equivalent to *backwards* because they start from the possible goals.

Neither method has shown clear advantage over the other as far as overall efficiency is concerned. The forward method has the advantage of giving better control over the order in which we acquire data that may possibly satisfy the premises. The backwards method is better in that it enables the interpreter to get closer to the goals it wishes to reach, as it can apply only those rules which are relevant to these goals. It is, however, difficult to foresee in which order these rules will be applied.

In the forward mode, the interpreter will often loop through the set of rules in order to find the one to apply: the situation when more than one rule can be applied is the conflict situation described later. A rule that cannot be applied during one cycle may become applicable in a subsequent cycle because the facts may have changed in the meantime as a consequence of the application of some rule. The interpreters OPS[3] and SNARK,[4] for example, operate in this way.

In the backwards mode the interpreter always has an aim in view and studies those rules that can lead to this aim. When it finds that in the current state of its knowledge it cannot evaluate some clause in the premise of a rule, it sets this evaluation as a new goal, and goes on in this way until it reaches known data; EMYCIN[5] works in this way, with the additional possibility of including some forward linking: some rules can be tagged to show that they can be activated as soon as their conditions are satisfied, but their conclusions are not propagated more than one step ahead. PROSPECTOR[6] allows the two modes to be mixed: it requires the user to input initial data from which it sets up an ordering of the goals that are to be reached by forward deductions, and then, having displayed this ordered list, asks which goal is to be attacked first.

"Closed" engine or guided dialog?

The less sophisticated programs simply read the data at the start of the session, perform the reasoning operations on these and give the result, without taking any advantage of the interactive possibilities offered by the computer. This is what I call a closed engine.

All future expert systems using the formalism of production rules will need to have some capacity for understanding natural language so as to be able to converse comfortably with their users. A first step in this direction will be to provide the program with the ability to conduct the dialog in a natural language; it will expect to get responses whose content is confined to the subject of the current question, and therefore will not need to undertake complex analyses of these responses. One way to improve the conversational style is to allow the interpreter to interpolate a question whenever it finds that it needs more information, rather than to go painstakingly through a standard list; this results in a dialog that can be rated as intelligent to the extent that a question put by the program is evidence of its "thinking" about the information it has and "realizing" that something is missing.

Strategies for conflict resolution

The term "conflict resolution" refers to the behavior of the interpreter in a situation where several rules could be applied; it has then to decide whether or not to apply them in some particular order and whether to apply all that are applicable or only some selection.

The problem of ordering the rules presents itself at several levels. At the top level the system can set an order in which they are to be applied, and the principle most commonly adopted with systems that use likelihood measures is that the ordering is in decreasing order of the strength of the conclusions or of the premises. There can also be some classification of the rules by hand as they are put into the system, but this is not to be recommended on method-ological grounds because it can reduce the modularity which is normally a valuable property of a formal system. However, the developer of the system may have good reasons for doing this in particular cases where the efficiency of the system does not take precedence over its ability to evolve; but the principle of aiming for modularity still holds and states that after a rule has been applied any other can be triggered.

The modularity is not affected if the ordering of the rules is done by the system because it is then the system itself that decides the correct place for each new rule. This procedure is of course valuable only if the applicable rules at any given stage are found not by an exhaustive search but after considering the most important; such a strategy can be regarded as "intelligent behavior" since the choice of a criterion on which to base a decision is evidence of a more complex reasoning process than a blind search through all the possibilities—taking it as agreed that one of the criteria for intelligence is the ability to deal with complexity (where complexity is necessary: recall Einstein's dictum, "Things should be made as simple as possible, but no simpler".)

But we should always be alive to the possible dangers of a strategy of non-exhaustive search in circumstances in which the information is not 100% certain, where inconsistencies between data items are frequent and there is no possibility of identifying erroneous data. Thus suppose we accept an output such as "Diagnostic D12 applies" without examining all the data but simply because the measure of D12's likelihood just exceeds a certain threshold; we are then open to the risk of a further data item arriving which will have the effect of lowering this measure so that it falls below that threshold. This problem is considered later in connection with the program LITHO (Chapter 17) for interpreting geological data, where one cannot have complete confidence in the information.

Another criterion for ordering the rules is to give priority to those that have been used most frequently; in circumstances in which statistics are compiled to show the relative frequencies of use of the different rules this can be valuable as suggesting those that might be "forgotten" because they are never used. But this fails to distinguish between two cases. Some rules will be used only rarely because the circumstances in which they are applied occur only rarely: they must be retained in spite of this, because they represent the very case that brought particular fame to a certain specialist. Others will be seldom or never be used because they have been badly expressed, or are useless because, for example, their conclusions are never used. A careful and detailed examination of the way in which the rules are linked in the reasoning process will usually reveal rules of this second type, which can then be eliminated.

Does or does not allow quantified variables?

In Chapter 9 the important distinction was made between propositional and predicate logic. The extra power of predicate logic comes from its use of quantified variables: thus the proposition "All birds have beaks" can be expressed in the language of first-order predicate logic but not in propositional logic, for in the latter it would be necessary to state explicitly that each individual bird had a beak.

Propositional logic can be adequate in the many cases in which only a single entity and its properties are being considered; this is so with many of the present-day expert systems, where the unique object of the study is for example a patient (for a medical diagnosis system) or a well (for a geological system). Even so a need for variables can arise, as for example in the case of the well where, in order to discuss details, it may be necessary to divide the single entity into a number of zones at different depths. As another example consider a program that "knows" Ohm's law $V = RI$ and which, whenever it has the values of two of the variables, decides to calculate the third. A comparison of the two representations shows the difference in power of the two formalisms:

Propositional calculus	**Predicate calculus**
R1: *if* V known & R known & I unknown	There is a formula f in which
then calculate I = V/R	*if* x unknown & y known &
R2: *if* V known & I known & R unknown	z known
then calculate R = V/I	*then* calculate x using
R3: *if* I known & R known & V unknown	f, y and z
then calculate V = RI	**Formulae**
	Y = RI
	P = VI etc. . . .

Ability to combine items of uncertain information

A large part of human reasoning is inductive in nature; a set of observations suggests an hypothesis, and as further observations become available either our confidence in this is increased progressively or it is shown to be untenable. Some production-rule formalisms allow weights to be introduced, indicating the confidence that can be placed in provisional conclusions. Such weights are often called *plausibilities:* I have deliberately avoided using the name "probability" because this has a specific statistical meaning, and also because the plausibilities that are used are often not at all objective but represent, for example, the experience of an expert in the field who is prepared to assign weights to rare events although he has no statistical knowledge concerning these.

A simple (but specific) example

The following example uses a rule base that describes various animals or classes of animal in terms of certain characteristics; the aim is to identify the animal or animals corresponding to a given description. The rule base has been made deliberately incorrect and incomplete, in order to illustrate the possibilities for improvement in such systems; at the same time, it is somewhat unrealistic in that the conclusions it reaches are not in fact very certain: there should be some means for taking into account weights that would represent the plausibilities of the various statements. Unfortunately, examples that use weak inferences and are both realistic and interesting are difficult to present in full because they soon involve appeal to many rules to which the conclusions are linked.

The example is specified completely by a rule base, an algorithm that defines the interpreter and the initial facts; a reader having zoological interests should consult more serious works on the subject.

Rule base
R1. *if* suckles-young *then* mammal
R2. *if* has-feathers *then* bird
R3. *if* has-fur *or* mammal *then* lives-in-forest
R4. *if* bird *and* does-not-fly *and* does-not-live-in-forest *then* penguin
R5. *if* lives-in-forest *and* very-heavy *then* bear
R6. *if* very-heavy *and* mammal *then* whale

Interpreter
1. find all rules for which the premise is TRUE (PATTERN MATCHING)
2. if there is more than one such rule, ignore any that duplicate a property already known (CONFLICT RESOLUTION)
3. perform the action required by the rule with the lowest serial number. If none, then stop ("ACTION")
4. repeat

Initial facts
FACTS = {suckles-young, very heavy}
POSSIBLE GOALS = {bear   whale   penguin}

The strategy given for the interpreter is the simplest that could be imagined: it scans the rule base continuously, selects a rule to apply (taking note of the condition that this must not affect a conclusion that has already been established) and initiates the corresponding action.

The process consists of a number of iterations through the steps of the algorithm.

Iteration 1: Only R1 is applicable, giving MAMMAL to be added to the facts base which thus becomes

FACTS = {suckles-young, very-heavy, mammal}

Iteration 2: R1, R3, R6 are applicable; R1 is rejected because it duplicates a property already known, so R3 is selected because it has the lowest serial number. This gives

FACTS = {suckles-young, very-heavy, mammal, lives-in-forest}

Iteration 3: R1, R3, R5, R6 are applicable; R1, R3 are rejected and R5 selected; then

    FACTS = {suckles-young, very-heavy, mammal, lives-in-forest, bear}

Iteration 4: R6, which has been delayed for a long time, is now executed and the system halts. The conclusion is

    FACTS = {suckles-young, very-heavy, mammal, lives-in-forest, bear, whale}

We notice straightaway that because the rule base does not provide sufficient logical discrimination we have two animals that fit the initial description; and it is easily seen that the characterization of the whale is seriously incomplete. Further, there are probably mammals other than the bear that are very heavy and live in forests, and there should be rules to identify these. Here it is R6 that is responsible for the ambiguous conclusion and all that is needed to resolve this ambiguity is an additional clause in its premise, thus

R6. *if* very-heavy *and* mammal *and* lives-in-water *then* whale

If this change is made and the program re-run the only difference will be that R6 will now not be executed, and the unique conclusion will be BEAR. R3 however is not strictly correct (for the reasons just given) and should be changed.

The lesson to be learned from this example is that a program can be modified simply by changing (and improving) the declarative part—for which there are editors in almost all high-level languages—and without the need usually encountered in traditionally-written programs for searching for an instruction that is hidden in the depths of the program.

Use of plausibility measures in uncertain reasoning

Purely deductive methods are not in fact very well adapted to real-life problems, for there the data are often uncertain and the inferences, which reflect expert opinion, are usually uncertain. Several methods have been developed to take these uncertainties into account with the aid of measures of the uncertainties associated with plausible inferences; the different methods are all more or less equivalent, in the sense that the different classifications they give of the plausibilities associated with the various statements are broadly the same, even if there are slight differences among the detailed results.

The Bayesian approach, described in Chapter 16, is often used by statisticians; here I shall describe the method used in EMYCIN:[5] a part of the medical diagnosis system MYCIN and itself a software tool used in constructing expert systems. There are good comparative studies of the different methods in the articles by Edward Shortliffe,[7] Bruce Buchanan and Dick Duda[8] and Henri Prade.[9]

The basis of the method is to assign to each statement a measure of likelihood or confidence lying between 1 (indicating complete confidence, meaning certainty that the statement is TRUE), and -1 (meaning certainty that it is FALSE); 0 indicates complete uncertainty. The value 0.2 is taken as the threshold above which it is reasonable to accept the truth of the statement, and -0.2 the corresponding threshold below which its falsity can reasonably be accepted. The likelihood of a statement A is written $v(A)$; it follows that if there is a rule $A = = > B$, which will have some likelihood value, and if $v(A) = 0.3$ for example, the likelihood of B from this rule alone cannot be greater than 0.3.

Uncertain premises. Suppose there is a rule R: A & B & C $= = > D$, with $v(R) = 0.8$, and that $v(A) = 0.4$, $V(B) = 0.6$, $v(C) = 0.7$; the plausibility of the premise (because A, B and C are related by a logical "and") is

$$v(\text{premise}) = \min [v(A), v(AB), v(C)] = 0.4$$

and therefore of the conclusion, using R, is

$$v(D) = 0.8 \times 0.4 = 0.32$$

Combination of information items. Suppose a statement D has an initial plausibility V1 and that further information gives it a plausibility V2; the resultant plausibility is then found (in EMYCIN) from

$$V = V1 + V2 - V1.V2 \text{ if } V1, V2 \text{ are both positive} \tag{1}$$
$$= V1 + V2 + V1.V2 \text{ if } V1, V2 \text{ are both negative} \tag{2}$$
$$= \frac{V1 + V2}{1 - \min(|V1|, |V2|)} \text{ if } V1, V2 \text{ have opposite signs} \tag{3}$$

Thus the initial plausibility can be either increased or decreased by the arrival of new information.

Rules (1) and (2) are simply extensions to the formulae for the composition of probabilities to allow for negative values. The justification for Rule (3) is that it increases the difference between positive and negative values. It had been customary in these circumstances to use the simple sum: V $= V1 + V2$. The group working on EMYCIN commented that if one had five reasons to believe that $V(E) = 0.9$ (from which it follows, by applying formula (1) four times, that the resultant plausibility is 0.99) and a single reason for believing $V(E) = -0.9$, the simple sum would give 0.09, meaning that the single negative reason had virtually cancelled all the other reasons; the new formula gives a very different result:

$$V = (0.99-0.90)/(1-0.90) = 0.90$$

Thus the difference between positive and negative values in the vicinity of 1 has been accentuated.

It should be noted here that

(a) the weights or plausibilities attached to the inferences are numbers provided by the expert in the subject; there may be some statistical justification for these values but in many cases they are expressions of his expertise, with no statistical basis;

(b) the above formulae for combining plausibilities are simply approximate representations of subjective reasoning, and have no mathematical justification.

There can be few people who, faced with the need to make a decision, have not listed the points "for" and "against" (so far as they can identify these) and decided according to the longer list. It is this type of reasoning that is simulated here, although with the refinement that different weights can be assigned to different criteria.

There is another method of attack on this problem that takes into account not the uncertainty of the data but their imprecision. This uses the concept of "fuzzy set", originated by Zadeh.[10] As the name implies, a fuzzy set is a set for which the boundary is not sharp but for which the change from membership to non-membership is gradual—such as the set of beautiful women, of small cars or the property of being young. The degree to which an object x can be regarded as belonging to a set E is measured by a function μE; thus if E is defined by the concept "is old" and if x is an individual's age, we could say

$$\mu E(1) = 0, \mu E(2) = 0, \mu E(3) = 0, E(4) = 0.1$$
$$\ldots \mu E(20) = 0.3, \ldots \mu E(50) = 0.7 \ldots \mu E(100) = 1$$

As the reader will of course have observed, the idea of "youth" or "age" depends very much on who is speaking and it is rather arbitrary to assign values out of context: after all, a young academic will be much older than an old cheese.

The fuzzy set concept has been applied in several programs, for example in medicine[11] and in mineral geology; in the latter, the PROSPECTOR[6] expert system includes in its process for approximate reasoning not only the degree of uncertainty associated with a fact (as is standard) but also the extent to which a given value for a property departs from the central value that is accepted as characterizing the object in question. This approach is not uncommon in medicine: thus whilst there may be a "normal" range within which, say, blood pressure should lie, a value slightly outside this range may be acceptable as "normal" in some circumstances.

Notes and references

[1] Post E. (1943), "Formal reductions of the general combinatorial decision problem", *American Journal of Mathematics,* 65, pp. 197-268.

[2] Chomsky N. (1957), *Syntactic structures,* La Haye, Mouton.

[3] Forgy C., McDermott J. (1977), "OPS a domain-independent production system language", *IJCAI 77,* pp. 933-939.

[4] Laurière J. L. (1982), "Représentation des connaissances", *RAIRO/TSI* Vol. 1 n° 2, pp. 109-133.

[5] Van Melle W. (1980), "A domain-independent system that aids in constructing knowledge-based consultation program", *Stanford Heuristic Programming Project memo,* HPP-80-22.

[6] Duda R., Gaschnig J., Hart P. (1979), "Model design in the Prospector consultant system for mineral exploration", in *Expert Systems in the microelectronic age,* Michie (ed.), Edinburgh, University of Edinburgh Press.

[7] Shortliffe E. H., Buchanan B. G. (1975), "A model of inexact reasoning in medicine", *Mathematical Biosciences 23,* pp. 351-379.

[8] Buchanan B. G., Duda R. O. (1982), "Principles of rule-based systems", *Stanford University technical report,* HPP-82-14.

[9] Prade H. (1983), "A synthetic view of approximate reasoning techniques", *IJCAI-83,* pp. 130-136.

[10] Zadeh L. A. (1978), "Fuzzy sets as a basis for a theory for possibility", *Fuzzy sets and systems,* New York, North-Holland.

[11] Sanchez E., Soula G. (1983), "Possibilistic analysis of fuzzy modelling in medicine", in *Modelling and data analysis in biotechnology and medical engineering,* Vansteenkiste and Young (eds.), Amsterdam, North-Holland Publishing Company.

13
Structured Objects

". . . I was half way between grasping the general concept of a horse and recognizing an individual horse; and at any rate, my knowledge of the horse in general had been provided by the outline, which was distinctive. If you see something from a great distance and have no idea of what it might be, you are content to describe it simply as a shape. When it has come closer you can say that it is an animal, even though you may not be able to say whether it is a horse or a donkey; and when it is closer still you will be able to say that it is indeed a horse, although you may not be able to say whether it is Brunel or Favel. Only when it is at the right distance will you be able to say that it is Brunel—that is, to say that it is one particular horse rather than another, whatever you have decided to call that horse."

Umberto Eco[1]

Introduction

The use of structured objects as a means of representation stemmed from the coming together of ideas generated in a number of different lines of research. These objects have been given a wide variety of names, such as the following:

— "Schemas", by the psychologist Bartlett[2] in his work on memory.
— "Frames", by Minsky[3] in the seminal paper in which he describes the process of understanding images and natural languages; and subsequently in several languages such as FRL[4] and UNITS.[5]
— "Scripts" by Schank and Abelson[6] which describe the relations between events in standard situations (see Chapter 8).
— "Prototypes" or "units" in the language KRL conceived by Bobrow and Winograd,[7] who use the work of Rosch[19] on categorization of concepts.
— "Objects" in many languages, for example SMALLTALK,[8] LOOPS,[20] FLAVORS,[9] ORBIT,[10] FORMES,[11] and MERING.[12]

I shall use the term "object", for various reasons; for one thing, it is general enough to cover the connotations of all the others, and for another the main rival "frame", though much used by American workers, has lost much of the richness of the concept that it had when originally proposed by Minsky.

Characteristics of structured objects

First, a number of technical terms that are in common use in this field. An object has a number of ASPECTS or ATTRIBUTES, which are the names of properties that characterize the object: thus a CIRCLE has a CENTER and a RADIUS, and PERSONAL-DETAILS of an individual will include NAME, AGE, SEX, ADDRESS, PROFESSION. Each ASPECT can have a number of distinct FACETS, some of which will be standard: one can be POSSIBLE-VALUES, giving the set of values that the ASPECT can take; another is DEFAULT, giving the value or values to be taken when no POSSIBLE-VALUES have been specified—for example, for the object CAR an ASPECT could be TOP-SPEED with a DEFAULT value of some number between 70 and 120 miles per hour. An object can be located at some point in a hierarchy, with other objects above and below it in the hierarchy, implying greater or less generality: thus BIRD is less general than ANIMAL but more general than CANARY.

A structured object can be regarded as a *prototype,* meaning an ideal with which to compare the objects that are being studied; this comparison will generally reveal differences, although there may be fundamental properties in common; and these differences may be genuine exceptions to the norm—as for example is the ostrich, as a bird that does not fly—or simply the specifying of details that were not provided for the ideal. This latter type of comparison of an object with the prototype has been much used in diagnosis, including medical: the influenza from which a particular patient is suffering will accord broadly with the prototype for influenza, but will have aspects that are peculiar to that patient.

Most representations by structured objects allow the specification of default values to be used when no other relevant information is available; and a default value can be replaced by an actual value if this becomes known at some later stage. Reasoning of this type, generally known as non-monotonic,[13] is important in human mental activity and cannot be expressed by pure first-order logic (see Chapter 9).

In the discussion of procedural systems it was pointed out that there were many advantages in expressing knowledge in declarative form, but that some actions were better expressed as programs. Representation by objects enables the two forms to be mixed, by giving the necessary procedural information with certain attributes of the objects. The language KRL[7] provides procedures of two types. There are what are called "domestic" procedures that state what should be done in order to perform certain operations successfully, such as finding the value of some attribute—an example in which the object is DATE is given later; and there are "demons", procedures that are activated whenever certain conditions are satisfied—this is nothing new, for the idea of "demon"[14] has been current in AI for a long time. This fairly standard mixing of declarative and procedural modes is found also in representation by semantic networks, where the difference between the two has not perhaps been made very clear so far.

Several writers maintain that it is important to be able to look at an event from different points of view. Thus Bobrow and Winograd, in KRL, give an example of an event that can be regarded either as a visit to a person or as a journey; in the first case the interest centres on the people involved, in the second on the destination and the method of transport.

There is no general method for deciding whether or not a prototype is a sufficiently close model of a situation that is to be identified. Usually some of the attributes that are considered important have the required values, but checks on other properties may lead to greater disparities between the ideal and the actual. It may be possible to state what action should be taken when the disparity becomes too great to be accepted: for example, if it were thought that a patient's symptoms were consistent with his having influenza, but he had a "loose cough", the possibility of bronchitis should be considered.

Some examples

Suppose we want to describe a rectangle by the four attributes length, breadth, position of center, color. For the first two attributes we can state the possible values as numbers, for the third that this is a point, and for the fourth that this is, say, red, yellow or blue; the description is then

```
(define RECTANGLE
     (length (value (a number)))
     (breadth (value (a number)))
     (center (value (a point)))
     (color (value (possibilities (red yellow blue)))))
```

We now consider some *main facets*.

1. *Value.* This states the value of an attribute, and can be a number, a character string, a list, an array, etc.

     e.g. (canary
            (color (value (yellow))))

2. *Default.* States the default value (if any) to be taken for the attribute in the absence of other information. It can be replaced by any other value without any problem of logical consistency arising.

    e.g. (chair
                (type (value furniture-item))
                (number-of-legs (default 4)))
          (grandmother's-chair
                (type (value chair))
                (number-of-legs 3))

Initially the object "grandmother's-chair" would be given the value 4 for the attribute "number-of-legs", by transmission of the default value from the parent object "chair"; this is replaced by the actual, and known, value 3.

3. *Constraints.* This is a list of predicates which, when given the values to be assigned to the aspects under consideration, must return TRUE, otherwise the assignment is not allowed.

    e.g. (age
                (constraints (greater-than 0)
                (less-than 150)))

4. *Possibilities.* This is a special case of CONSTRAINTS, where the set of possible values for an attribute is stated.

    e.g. (sex
                (possibilities (masculine feminine)))

In the last two cases, any attempt to assign a value that does not satisfy the conditions results in a message being output of the type "NEUTER is not a valid SEX".

5. *Interval.* Another way in which to express a constraint; if the constraint is numerical, maximum and minimum values are given.

    e.g. (age
                (interval (0 150)))

6. *Procedure.* This enables a function (written in LISP here) to be defined in order to compute the value of an aspect; this type of "procedural attachment" is called a domestic procedure in KRL.[7]

Consider for example the object DATE, having the aspects day, month, year and day-of-week. The last is easily calculated by means of a function that takes as its initial conditions the fact that 1 January 1900 was a Monday, and uses the facts that after each year the day of the week is shifted by 1 (mod 7) for the same date, provided that was not a leap year, and so on. Thus:

```
(date
    (day (interval (1 31)))
    (month (interval (1 12)))
    (year (interval (0 99)))
    (day-of-week
        (constraints (Monday Tuesday . . . Sunday))
        (procedure (compute-day-week
            (the day)
            (the month)
            (the year)))))
```

Here the word "the" acts as an auxiliary function that takes the values of day, month and year from the object that has been created and passes these to the procedure compute-day-week.

7. *Demon.* This specifies a function which should be carried out whenever the value of the corresponding attribute changes. Thus an object SIGNAL, which is able to take either of the colors RED, GREEN and cause a message to be sent out whenever the color changes, can be defined as follows:

```
(signal
    (color
        (constraints (red green))
        (demon (warning (the color)))))
```

where the function warning is defined.

```
(define warning (color)
    (print (select color)
        (red "machine busy")
        (green "machine free"))))
```

Hierarchies. A fundamental property of object-based languages is that they allow hierarchies of objects to be set up, and properties to be transmitted from parent objects to descendants if the required characteristic cannot be found at the level of the object under consideration. For example, suppose a series of objects are defined as follows:

```
(defobject bird
    (an animal)
    (characteristic "flies"))
(defobject canary
    (a bird)
    (color "yellow"))
```

```
(defobject Joey
   (a canary))
(defobject ostrich
   (a bird)
   (characteristic "does not fly"))
```

With the aid of a program in LISP the following dialog could be conducted; here U denotes the user, P the program.

dialog	comments
U: (characteristic ostrich)	found directly at level "ostrich"
P: does not fly	
U: (characteristic Joey)	not found at level "Joey" nor at "canary",
P: flies	but found at "bird"
U: (color Joey)	not found at level "Joey" but inherited
P: yellow	from "canary"

Notice that the characteristic of "ostrich" does not satisfy the general property of "bird".

Handling objects

We now consider the problem of recognizing an object (or identifying a situation) among a multiplicity of objects linked by a variety of relations which generally include hierarchies; what is required is to find the object that agrees with the specification provided, as closely and in as great detail as possible. Thus if the subject were medical diagnosis of cerebro-vascular irregularities in particular, it would be better to name an illness as thrombotic ischemia rather than simply as ischemia, since the former would account for the data (i.e., the symptoms) in greater detail.

Objects usually exist in one of three states (cf. Szolovits[15]):

Active—when the object is already on the list of current hypotheses, and its validity is being investigated.

Semi-active—the hypothesis has been suggested by several lines of reasoning, but not sufficiently strongly for it to be put on the current list.

Inactive—any hypothesis concerning the object that has been rejected or has not been considered.

The checking process is usually organized as follows:

(a) Input the initial data.
(b) Frame several hypotheses, using the rules relevant to the data.
(c) Arrange these hypotheses in some order.
(d) Test the hypotheses by assigning the aspects of the objects thus created. New facts may be inferred from those already available and

new hypotheses put forward, with a possible return to step (b) if it is found that the current hypothesis should be replaced by another. As with rule-based systems, questions may be asked during the process of attempting to assign values.

(e) After all the hypotheses have been examined, if there are several contenders for acceptance some provisional policy may be devised for discriminating between these.

(f) The best choice is output, or choices if several meet this criterion.

Reasoning from incomplete information, and by default

Most human reasoning processes can work despite the absence of complete information; this lack does not hold up the thinking. Research into simulation of our reasoning in such circumstances has shown up the inadequacy of such techniques as decision trees, which are defeated by missing information because this prohibits the choice of the next branch to follow. Hence, as Reiter[16] has remarked, all the methods developed for AI include a more or less explicit rule that states, "If a wanted piece of information cannot be deduced from the knowledge base, then . . ."

The problem of reasoning by default is essentially that of dealing with exceptions. The majority of facts about the real world are of the form "most Ps are Qs", or "most Ps have the property Q"; thus the statement "most birds fly" means "all birds fly except the ostrich, the penguin . . .".

Because of the *necessity* for the system to be logically valid, any program based on first-order predicate calculus must list explicitly *all* the exceptions to any statement; so the above statement must be written

$$(\forall\ X)\ BIRD(X) \land \neg OSTRICH(X) \land \neg PENGUIN(X) \implies FLIES(X)$$

This, however, does not allow us to conclude that birds in general fly: to prove that a given bird X flies the program must achieve the intermediate goals

X is not an OSTRICH and X is not a PENGUIN

which is impossible if no more precise information is given than "X is a BIRD".

Programs using first-order logic usually include a rule "If x is an individual and if $\neg P(x)$ cannot be deduced from the data, then assume $P(x)$"—which is not a concept of first-order logic. This rule is incorporated into PROLOG[17] by means of the operator NOT, and into MICRO-PLANNER[18] by THNOT. A language that does not include such a rule cannot be viable, for without it a prohibitive number of negative facts would have to be given explicitly in the program.

Notes and references

[1] Eco U. (1982), *Le nom de la rose,* Paris, Grasset.

[2] Bartlett F. (1932), *Remembering, a study in experimental and social psychology,* London, Cambridge University Press.

[3] Minsky M. (1975), "A framework for representing knowledge", in P. Winston (ed.), *The psychology of computer vision,* New York, McGraw-Hill.

[4] Roberts B., Goldstein I. (1977), "The FRL manual", *MIT AI Laboratory Memo 409,* September 1977. (FRL = Frame Representation Language).

[5] Stefik, M. (1979), "An examination of a frame-structured representation system" *IJCAI-79,* Tokyo.

[6] Schank R., Abelson R. (1977), *Scripts, plans, goals and understanding,* Lawrence Erlbaum Ass., Hillsdale, NJ.

[7] Bobrow D., Winograd T. (1977), "KRL, another perspective", *Cognitive Science 3,* pp. 29-42. (KRL = Knowledge Representation Language).

[8] Kay A., Goldberg A. (1977), "Personal dynamic media", *Computer 10,* pp. 31-410.

[9] Moon D. A., Weinreb D. (1980), "FLAVORS: message-passing in the Lisp machine", MIT, *AI memo 602.*

[10] Steels L. (1982), "An applicative view of object-oriented programming", *European Conference on Integrated Interactive Computing Systems,* Stresa, Italy.

[11] Cointe P., Rodet X. (1983), "FORMES: a new object-language for managing a hierarchy of events", *IFIP-83,* Paris.

[12] Ferber J. (1984), "MERING: un langage d'acteur pour la représentation des connaissances et la compréhension du langage naturel", *4ᵉ Congrès de Reconnaissance des formes et intelligence artificielle,* Paris, pp. 179-189.

[13] McDermott D., Doyle J. (1980), "Non-monotonic logic I", *Artificial Intelligence,* Vol. 13, 1 & 2, pp. 41-72.

[14] Selfridge O. (1959), "Pandemonium, a paradigm for learning", *Symposium on mechanization of thought processes,* National Physical Laboratory, Teddington, England.

[15] Szolovits P., Pauker S. G. (1978), "Categorical and probabilistic reasoning in medical diagnosis", *Artificial Intelligence,* 11, pp. 115-144.

[16] Reiter R. (1978), "On reasoning by default", *Theoretical issues in Natural Language Processing-2,* University of Illinois.

[17] Roussel P. (1975), *PROLOG, manuel de référence et d'utilisation,* Groupe d'Intelligence Artificielle, Marseille.

[18] Hewitt C., (1972), "Description and theoretical analysis (using schemata) of PLANNER: A language for proving theorems and manipulating models in a robot", *AI memo 271,* MIT.

[19] Rosch E. (1975), "Cognitive representations of semantic categories", *Journal of Experimental Psychology,* 1975, 104, pp. 192-233.

[20] Bobrow D., Stefik M. (1983), *The LOOPS manual,* Xerox PARC, Palo Alto.

14
Programs for Playing Chess and Solving Problems

Chess-playing programs

Many people look on writing programs for playing chess or bridge as a frivolous activity; but this is usually evidence of an inability to appreciate that there is a great deal of interest in analyzing, and looking for means of representing, every aspect of human reasoning. Research on chess-playing programs has in fact led to the discovery of efficient algorithms for searching trees, because such structures are those most commonly used now to represent the sequence of possible moves in a game (see Fig. 14.2). Further, the cognitive processes brought into play in a game such as chess are often the same as those of other activities that are considered more serious, and the strategies developed are of the same nature as those in any situation where adversaries face each other and aim to see their own plans succeed and their opponents' defeated.

Constructing chess-playing programs was one of the earliest interests of AI researchers; the first ideas on this were conceived by Claude Shannon[1] as far back as 1949 when the name "artificial intelligence" had not been invented. Shannon proposed a system for representing the 64 squares on the board and also a set of values for the different pieces (Queen = 9, Rook = 5, Bishop = 3, Knight = 3, Pawn = 1), with which to evaluate any possible position, taking into account both the mobility of the pieces (the number of legal moves available) and the dispositions of the pawns (giving negative points for isolated pawns or pawns doubled on the same rank). His suggestion for attacking the problem consisted of considering, at each position, all possible moves for the player whose turn it was; then all possible replies by the opponent; then all possible replies to those moves, and so on; evaluating a function designed to represent the "value" of each potential position; and finally choosing the move that led to the best position, for the player, at some later stage on the tree structure thus developed.

Shannon's successors introduced new criteria in order to improve the value function. Richard Greenblatt,[2] of MIT, suggested a parameter that would encourage the player who had numerical superiority, but only that player, to exchange pieces; and another that would measure the relative safeties of the two kings. Further criteria have been introduced since then, such as control of the center and the possibilities for attack; however, the importance of these will vary during the course of the game, the relative security of the kings, for example, becoming less important as the major pieces are removed from the board.

When it was first proposed, producing a program that would play chess was considered a stiff challenge,[3] and it is still regarded as a problem in artificial intelligence, although the commercially-available programs of 1984 have very little in common with the working of human reasoning. The combinatorial explosion here is on such a scale that there is no possibility of an exhaustive search through all the positions that could be reached; so the problem is rather to find an acceptable solution, meaning the best that can be found within the limited time available, in spite of the search being necessarily incomplete. The impossibility of the exhaustive search is made clear by the fact that with an average game involving 80 single moves the total number of possible positions is of the order of 10^{120}.

If Shannon's method is programmed in the classical way, the choice of the next move is decided by evaluating the tree of possible moves down to some specified depth, the program making the assumption that at each node the player whose turn it is will choose the branch that is "best" for him. Here "best" is usually defined by means of a fixed value function. If it is White to play and the function is such that a high value means an advantage to White, the program must choose the branches so as to maximize the function at the odd nodes (White to play) and minimize it at the even nodes (Black to play): this is the *minimax*[4] algorithm.

The chessboard notation used here is shown in Fig. 14.1. As a very simple example, suggested by Frey[5], consider the opening moves shown in Fig. 14.2, with, as is usual, White to move. Only a few of the possible moves are considered, such as those of the Queen's pawn or the King's pawn, and the tree is evaluated to a depth of 4, representing 2 moves each for White and Black. The nodes are marked with a square or a circle according to whether it is White's move or Black's, respectively, and are numbered in the order in which they are examined, the strategy being "depth first", meaning that a

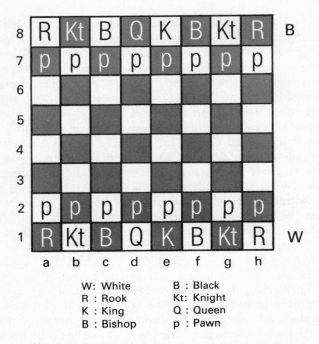

W: White   B : Black
R : Rook   Kt: Knight
K : King   Q : Queen
B : Bishop   p : Pawn

Figure 14.1   Chess: names of pieces, board notation

branch once chosen is followed to the maximum depth before another is taken up.

Thus the program examines these moves:

1. Pawn $e_2 - e_4$ Pawn $e_7 - e_5$
2. Knight $g_1 - f_3$ Knight $b_8 - c_6$

computes the final value at position (5) and stores the result, $+1$. It then continues:

1. Pawn $e_2 - e_4$ Pawn $e_7 - e_5$
2. Knight $g_1 - f_3$ Pawn $d_7 - d_6$

leading to the value $+1$ for position (6); and so on until all 17 terminals on the graph have been evaluated. After a node has been evaluated the value is returned to the node above (its immediate parent) and remains the value for that node until displaced by a better (i.e., greater) value arising from another descendant. This continues until all[6] the nodes, to the planned depth, have been evaluated and the move that maximizes the value function is selected.

As will be appreciated, the best programs use complex value functions; but as an example consider the following very simple form. At a given position let LW, LB be the number of legal moves for white and black

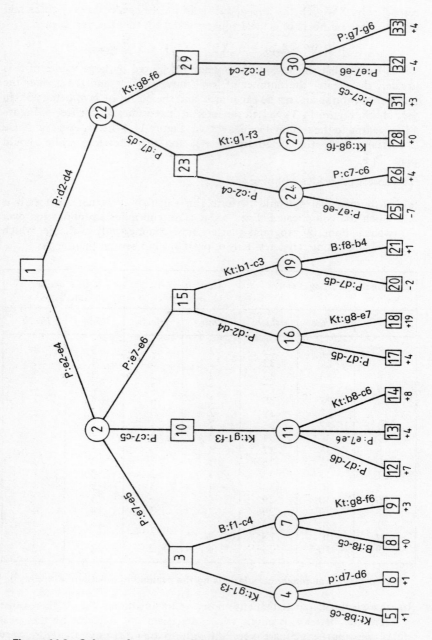

Figure 14.2 Sub-tree for two possible opening moves by White (*from Frey[5]*)

respectively, XW, XB the least numbers of moves needed to give check and CW, CB the numbers of central squares attacked; the function is then

$$f = (LW - LB) + 3(XB - XW) + 3(CW - CB)$$

which means that the advantage to white (measured by large values of f) is greater, the greater the number of legal moves he has and the greater the number of central squares he can attack, and the nearer he is to being able to give check. Figure 14.3 gives all the intermediate values for the tree of Figure 14.2, leading to the terminal values shown. Figure 14.4 then shows that Node 2 corresponds to the maximum of +1, and that therefore white should play P: $e_1 - e_4$

The observant reader will note that

(a) no human player would perform this calculation during a game: it is much too complicated. Even so, it is an enormous simplification over what is done by programs that are now commercially available, which evaluate not merely a few tens of positions but several thousands;

Terminal position	Legal moves		Moves to check		Center squares attacked	
	White	Black	White	Black	White	Black
5	27	29	2	3	3	3
6	27	32	2	3	3	2
8	33	33	2	2	2	2
9	33	27	2	2	2	2
12	27	29	2	4	3	2
13	27	29	2	3	3	2
14	27	25	2	4	3	3
17	38	34	3	3	3	3
18	38	22	3	3	3	2
20	33	35	3	3	3	3
21	31	33	3	2	3	1
25	30	34	4	3	3	3
26	30	29	4	4	3	2
28	29	29	3	3	4	4
31	30	24	4	3	3	3
32	30	28	4	2	3	3
33	30	23	4	2	3	2

Figure 14.3   Preliminary calculations by the evaluating function (*after Frey*[5])

(b) there is no guarantee that any chosen value function is "best": there must certainly be considerations which are taken into account by the great players but which are very difficult to quantify and therefore very difficult to incorporate into a value function.

Node	Value from Min(f)	Node	Value from Max(f)	Node	Value from Min(f)	Node	Value from Max(f)
4	+ 1	13	+ 1				
7	0						
11	+ 4	10	+ 4	2	+ 1		
16	+ 4	15	+ 4				
19	− 2					1	+ 1
24	− 7	23	0				
27	0			22	− 4		
30	− 4	29	− 4				

Figure 14.4   Evaluation taken to the root of the tree of Figure 14.2 (after Frey[5])

The first to attack the difficulty represented by (a) was Jacques Pitrat[7] of the University of Paris VI; he, and later Wilkins,[8] introduced the idea of high-level STRATEGIES as a means for pruning the tree. This made it possible to ignore all but a number of "promising" branches, where "promise" was defined in terms of a stated GOAL that was to be attained. Such a goal might be, for example, "take such-and-such an opposing piece" or "put the opposing King in check"; the program would set up sub-goals whose achievement would lead to the main goal. A program using such a strategy can look twenty or more moves ahead, which it certainly could not do in an exhaustive search, because it need examine only those moves that would lead to certain sub-goals.

The form of the strategy to be developed will be dictated by the nature of the main GOAL to be achieved. Suppose for example the program chooses the protection of its King as its main GOAL: it will find several ways of reducing the threat to the King, one of which is to attack the opposing Queen—this can be sub-goal 1. To achieve this the program may find that it should move either the Knight or the Bishop; suppose it chooses the Bishop's move as sub-goal 2. It may then appear that such a move would leave a Pawn unsupported, and therefore that before making the move another Pawn should be advanced so as to support the one now protected by the Bishop—this is taken as sub-goal 3; and so on.

The trees thus developed are much narrower than those of the exhaustive search but much deeper, and the number of positions examined is reduced from tens of thousands to a few hundreds or even a few tens; the program thus begins to work more along the lines of the human player. A consequence of this type of approach is that a number of successive moves are linked by a strategy, in contrast to the blind search in which nothing links two consecutive moves because the entire tree has to be re-evaluated as a result of the conditions having changed. Any resemblance to strategic behavior is then a matter of pure chance.

The need to have a value function, for lack of anything better, arises of course because something has to replace the eye of the human player which can take in the entire situation in a few seconds' glance at the board. Making the program depend on such functions is not necessarily the best principle, and it is very likely that there is much to be gained in future by reducing their importance in favor of heuristic methods obtained from the best players. Moreover, if programs can be written whose play is more and more like that of the masters, these will help to give a better understanding of the strategies used by the best players.

A further comment is that success in producing programs that play at a high level of skill would be of more general importance in AI, apart from chess: it would lead to a better understanding of the concept of a *plan*, which enters equally into the understanding of natural language. It often happens that we cannot really understand an account of some event without some knowledge of the motivations of the participants, which will explain their actions in terms of plans they might have made.

Finally, it is interesting to recall that a program for playing backgammon written by Hans Berliner[9] beat the world champion. Berliner himself admitted that his program had good luck, because at each turn the play depends on the throw of the dice; and a deep study made after the game showed that 8 out of its 73 moves were not optimal. This was in fact a unique event in the history of AI; and some of the program's methods for evaluating the positions can be generalised to apply to other problems.

Problem solving

One of our commonest intellectual activities is solving problems, which can range from questions like "how do I get from home to Birmingham?" to intelligence tests or the problem of the cannibals and the missionaries discussed later in this chapter.

1. Geometrical analogies

A standard type of problem included in intelligence tests is that in which a series of drawings is given, from which the solver has to discover the rule that transforms Drawing 1 into Drawing 2, and then which is the logical successor to Drawing 3. The following example was conceived by Evans[10] and Bundy.[11]

The method is first to find a verbal description for each drawing and to infer a rule that relates one description to the next; the rule will not always be found at the first attempt, for there are often several possibilities that have to be tested by seeing which apply also to the second transformation, and so on.

A symbolic representation of the verbal description must then be found, in terms of which the similarities and differences between the various draw-ings can be expressed. We ourselves carry out such a process unconsciously, but it has to be made explicit for the computer; it is equivalent to going from a phrase in natural language to its internal representation as a set of relations between verbs, nouns and so on.

Figure 14.5   What is D?

The verbal descriptions for the problem of Fig. 14.5 could be, for example:

A: A square with a ring on its perimeter
B: A square with a ring in its interior
C: A triangle with a ring on its perimeter.

The rule changing A into B is:

CHANGE "on its perimeter" into "in its interior"

which when applied to C gives:

D: A triangle with a ring in its interior.

The symbolic description can be constructed by defining predicates such as ON and IN, whose arguments are the objects in the figure; this gives:

A: (ON RING SQUARE)
B: (INTERIOR RING SQUARE)
C: (ON RING TRIANGLE)

The rule is then: A → B: CHANGE ON INTERIOR and if this is applied to C the result is

D: (INTERIOR RING TRIANGLE)

The capacity for recognizing the similarities and differences between different situations is typical of the learning processes discussed in Chapter 19; it is of course fundamental to reasoning in general.

2.   *"Missionaries and cannibals" problem*

Three missionaries and three cannibals are together on the left bank (L) of a river and want to cross to the right bank (R); they have a boat that can carry only two people at a time. If at any stage, on either bank, there are more cannibals than missionaries the former's taste for human flesh gets the better of them with disastrous consequences for the latter, who seek to avoid this at all costs. When the boat is at one bank or the other it is considered as part of that bank. The problem is how to get everyone across the river, with the missionaries remaining safe. Daniel Kayser[16] commented to me that he couldn't see why two hungry cannibals shouldn't be able to finish off three well-fed missionaries: it would be a very intelligent program indeed that could make such an observation.

The AI problem is to write a program that will itself find what moves have to be made—who is to take the boat back and forth—so as to achieve the desired aim. For this, we have to give formal descriptions of the initial state, the final state to be attained and the state-change operators. The program must check that at all times the number of missionaries (M) exceeds the number of cannibals (C) on either bank or in the boat when that is in midstream, except when (M) = 0 in any of these locations.

We should note that in constructing the formal description of the problem we have effectively ignored the subtle process of going from the statement in natural language to the representation in terms of states and operators: this is in fact the most difficult part and implies a very deep understanding of language. The fact that, for example, "the cannibals' taste for human flesh gets the better of them . . . etc." implies that number (M) must exceed number (C), etc., would be a far from trivial deduction for a program.

This particular problem is simple enough for an exhaustive search to be feasible, that is, for the program to apply the various operators blindly, with the sole constraint that no state must ever be generated in which the cannibals outnumber the missionaries.

The formal definition of the problem is:

Initial state   L = (MMMCCC) (everyone on left bank)
                   R = 0
Final state   L = 0
                   R = (MMMCCC) (everyone on right bank)

A set of operators $O = (O_1, O_2, O_3, O_4, O_5)$ together with their definitions. Each operator results in a change of state and can be applied only under certain conditions. For example, the operator O_1 could be defined as follows:

ORIGIN = L or R
DESTINATION = L or R
CONDITIONS:
    ORIGIN ≠ DESTINATION
    n (M, ORIGIN) > 1   (at least one missionary and cannibal
                         at the origin)
    n (C, ORIGIN) > 1

RESULT:

ORIGIN ← ORIGIN − (CM)   description of new state

DESTINATION ← DESTINATION + (CM)

The complete program for this example is given in the book edited by Alan Bundy.[11]

The method just described has the drawback of being too specific to the particular problem and not generalizable to others; such considerations have led other workers to try to develop more general methods, such as Jean-Louis Laurière's ALICE.[12] The best known of such systems is GPS (General Problem Solver) conceived by Newell, Simon and Shaw.[13]

3. The GPS program

Here as with all problem-solving systems the initial and final states (the data and the goal respectively) must of course be specified and also the state-change operators; but now the operators can be more general because their sole aim is to reduce the difference between the current state and the goal. The method is one of "means and ends" and can be applied to a very wide range of problems.

If I want to solve the problem of how to get from my home, say in London, to Edinburgh, I look for an "operator" that will reduce the difference between the states "at home" and "in Edinburgh". This difference is one of distance and can be reduced by taking a plane or a train; these, however, start not from my home but from the airport or the railway station, so I have a new sub-goal, "get to the airport (or station)", which I must now plan to achieve, and so on. An important feature of a general program is that the operator chosen to reduce the difference between initial and final states may not be applicable to the object under consideration at the time, such as the plane or the train here; rather than reject an operator for this reason GPS tries to change the current object into one that is appropriate to the operator. The types of goals with which GPS can deal are:

1. Transform an object A into an object B
2. Reduce some difference between A and B by modifying A
3. Apply an operator to A

The most general version of GPS can solve 11 different types of problem, including puzzles and problems in particular fields such as chess and symbolic integration. In this last field its performance is much inferior to that of specialized systems such as MACSYMA[14] or SAINT.[15] But GPS was never intended to be efficient; rather, according to its authors, it should be regarded as "a series of studies aimed at giving a better view of the nature of the problem-solving process and of the mechanisms brought into play in order to reach a solution".

4. The ALICE program

This program, conceived by Jean-Louis Laurière[12] of the University of Paris VI, can solve logical and mathematical problems expressed in a language that uses the vocabulary of set theory and classical logic.

The statement of a problem is in four parts:

1. The definition part, prefaced by the word "LET"; this defines the objects that are the subject of the problem and specifies their types.
2. The goal part, prefaced with the word FIND; this states the values that have to be found.
3. The "constraint" part, prefaced with the word "WITH"; this gives the relations that must exist between the variables of the problem.
4. The data, which can be numerical or symbolic.

There are three main phases in the solution process:

(a) Propagation of the constraints, consisting in substituting in the given expressions the values that have been chosen for certain variables. It is here that ALICE shows its skill, by using the constraints not in a fixed order but according to some criteria such as those for which the expression is short before those for which it is long.
(b) Generation of hypotheses; choices are made as intelligently as possible by choosing the most probable values.
(c) Arriving at the solution and showing that it is optimal.

ALICE is particularly good at cryptarithmetical problems; for example

$$
\begin{array}{ccccccc}
  & G & E & R & A & L & D \\
+ & D & O & N & A & L & D \\
\hline
= & R & O & B & E & R & T
\end{array}
$$

where each of the letters G E R A L D O N B T represents one of the digits 0,1 . . 9, all are different and the sum is correct; the leading digits D G R are all non-zero.

If a, b, c, d, e are the carries in the addition, from left to right, ALICE generates the following relations which form the constraints for the problem:

$$
\begin{array}{rclcll}
 & 2D &=& T &+& 10e \quad (1) \\
e + & 2L &=& R &+& 10d \quad (2) \\
d + & 2A &=& E &+& 10c \quad (3) \\
c + R + & N &=& B &+& 10b \quad (4) \\
b + E + & O &=& O &+& 10a \quad (5) \\
a + G + & D &=& R & & \quad (6)
\end{array}
$$

The first inferences made by the program are:

T is even, by (1);
either (a = 0 & b = 0 & E = 0)

or (a = 1 & b = 1 & E = 9), by (5)
R = e (modulo 2) by (2)
E = d (modulo 2) by (3)
ALICE now makes the provisional choice E = 0 (implying a = b = 0) which changes the original constraints to the stronger forms:

$$d \ + \ 2A \ = \ 10c \qquad (3')$$
$$c \ + \ R \ + \ N \ = \ B \qquad (4')$$
$$G \ + \ D \ = \ R \qquad (6')$$

It follows from (3') that d is even and therefore, since it is a carry digit, d = 0. The process continues in this manner and the solution is found by developing a tree with only 6 nodes, as shown in Fig. 14.6. The "leaves" R = 4 and R = 6 lead to impossibilities when substituted in the other equations, so only R = 7 is acceptable; the solution is:

G	E	R	A	L	D	O	N	B	T
1	9	7	4	8	5	2	6	3	0

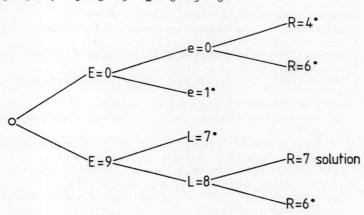

Figure 14.6   ALICE search tree for GERALD + DONALD = ROBERT

The complete program is given in Laurière's book.[12]

Conclusion

The study of problem solving in general has undoubtedly had an important influence on the development of inference engines for expert systems; such systems are the subject of Part IV of this book. The incorporation of high-level strategies, such as the concept of *plan*, into chess-playing programs is likely to bring benefits in the future.

Notes and references

[1] Shannon C. E. (1950), "Programming a computer to play chess", *Scientific American*, February 1950.

[2] Greenblatt R. D. et. al. (1967), "The Greenblatt chess program", *Proc. AFIPS Fall Joint Computer Conference*, 1967, 31, pp. 801-810.

[3] Even the possibility [of creating a good chess-playing program] was questioned by Dreyfus in his book *"What computers can't do: A critique of Artificial Reason"*, New York, Harper & Row, 1972. The challenge now is to produce a program that will play at Grandmaster level, or even world champion.

[4] Von Neuman J., Morgenstern O. (1944), *Theory of games and economic behavior*, Princeton N.J., Princeton University Press.

[5] Frey P. W. (ed.) (1977), *Chess skill in man and machine*, New York, Springer-Verlag.

[6] There are in fact tree-pruning methods that do not require all the nodes to be evaluated. The reader interested in these optimization procedures should consult, for example, Barr, A. & Feigenbaum E. (eds.) (1981), *The Handbook of Artificial Intelligence*, Vol. 1, 46-108, Los Altos, California, Kaufmann.

[7] Pitrat J. (1977), "A chess combination program which uses plans", *Journal of Artificial Intelligence*, Vol. 8, n° 3, June 1977.

[8] Wilkins D. (1979), "Using plans in chess", *IJCAI-79* pp. 960-967, Tokyo, August 1979.

[9] Berliner H. (1980), "Computer Backgammon", *Scientific American*, pp. 54-69, June 1980.

[10] Evans T. G. (1963), "A heuristic program to solve geometric analogy problems", in *Semantic Information Processing*, M. Minsky (ed.), Cambridge, Mass., MIT Press.

[11] Bundy A., Burstall R. M., Weir S., Young R. M. (1980), *Artificial Intelligence: An Introductory course*, Edinburgh, Edinburgh University Press.

[12] Laurière J. L. (1978), "A language and a program for stating and solving combinatorial problems", *Artificial Intelligence*, 10, 1, pp. 29-127.

[13] Ernst G., Newell A. (1969), GPS: *A case study in generality and problem solving*, New York, Academic Press.

[14] Moses J. (1967), "Symbolic integration", *Technical Report MAC-TR-47*, MIT.

[15] Slagle J. R. (1963), *A heuristic program that solves symbolic integration problems in freshman calculus*, Feigenbaum and Feldman (eds.), New York, McGraw-Hill.

[16] Kayser D. (1984), Personal letter.

Part Four

Expert Systems

15
Characteristics of Expert Systems

Introduction

The rise in interest in expert systems coincided with a fall in interest on the part of AI researchers in general methods of representation of reasoning. Methods intended to be universal, or fully general, had in fact proved to have too little power when applied in particular fields[1]—an illustration of the usual trade-off between generality and efficiency. In the early 1960s Edward Feigenbaum started to take an interest in reasoning methods that were inductive and empirical: a typical problem in which such methods would be used was that of devising the hypothesis that would best interpret a set of observed data. The wish to model this type of scientific behavior led to the setting up of a collaborative project[2] involving on the the one hand information scientists and on the other, experts in certain fields among whom was the chemist and geneticist Joshua Lederberg. The particular field chosen for experimentation was the interpretation of mass-spectrograph data: in a mass spectrograph a small sample of a substance whose chemical composition is to be found is bombarded with high energy electrons, with the result that the molecules are broken into many fragments and atoms migrate between these fragments; the original molecular structure can then be found from the results of examinations of the fragments. The DENDRAL[3] program written to attack this problem is described in Chapter 17.

This work, running counter to the dogma of general methods (dear to the mathematicians) then prevailing, was regarded with considerable reserve by the AI establishment for several years. But it soon caused the central problem of the representation and structuring of knowledge to be raised again, because now "real" problems were being attacked, not merely "toy" problems for which only a few parameters had to be taken into account.

The rise and fall in the importance of research fields is typical of the succession described by Thomas Kuhn in "The structure of scientific revolution".[4] He describes the evolution of science as a cyclic process in which "normal" periods alternate with "revolutions". During a normal period there is a fairly general consensus on what are the important questions to be studied and what types of answer or explanation are sought. The basis of the current theory, or model of the universe, is not questioned, and progress is made slowly within the bounds of this theory or model. After a time problems arise within these bounds that urgently demand attention; at first they are ignored, but a critical moment arrives after which an increasing number of researchers, dissatisfied with the existing model, start to lay the foundations for a new one. Within the bounds of this new model the previously unanswered questions become better understood but some phenomena may be less well explained than before; the new theory or model is thus not simply an extension of the old but a new basis for "normal" science, and of course is a source of dispute between the champions of the old and the advocates of the new.

Once it was recognized that research into reasoning mechanisms for particular fields had enabled great progress to be made, a new enthusiasm grew up for developing general tools to use in representing knowledge from different special fields; so research into expert systems could then be considered to form a valid part of artificial intelligence.

The first lesson learned from the construction of a program such as DENDRAL, which included an enormous amount of specialized chemical information, was that the cost of making the smallest modification was prohibitive. This was because the special knowledge was integrated into the mechanisms that used and interpreted it; gradually, therefore, the fundamental principle emerged that the knowledge base should be separated from the interpretation mechanism.

Principles of expert systems

1. Specifying the field. By its very nature the construction of an expert system is an incremental task necessitating many sessions with an expert in its particular field. The human expert will explain his/her knowledge and way of going about solving problems, probably in a somewhat disorganized fashion because this is probably the first time he/she has been asked to do such a thing. The expert must therefore be allowed to make many revisions of what he/she wants to be put into the program, with much backtracking, detailed explanation of certain points, and additions. This makes clear the need to separate the representation of the knowledge from the program that will apply it. In a second phase of the project other experts may be invited to comment on the information provided by the first, so this must be put into a form that is easy to read and study; the forms of representation described in Chapters 9 to 13 will be helpful for this purpose. These forms are essentially declarative and are not in the style of a classical programming language. Taking a long view, it can even be expected that in future the human experts themselves will produce the programs without the help of information scientists.

Figure 15.1 suggests an architectural structure that will enable a user to conduct a dialog with an expert system; it is not necessary to use this

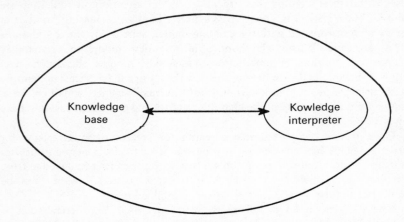

Figure 15.1   Underlying organization of an expert system

form, but it is in fact the one most commonly adopted. The real necessity is to have the collaboration of a true expert in the field. However, such a structure is made almost indispensable by the fact that the knowledge as provided will be a fairly random collection of items, and this will make classical programming methods inappropriate. If it is possible to put these items into an organized form it is likely that other, more classical, methods will be more suitable in this case than those of expert systems. Once a system has been developed to a stage at which its performance in its special field is considered satisfactory, its knowledge base can if necessary be integrated into the interpretation program, either for reasons of efficiency or to reduce the demands on memory, the latter perhaps to allow a commercial version to run on smaller computers than the one on which it was developed.

2.   *Explanation of the reasoning process.* Another important feature of expert systems is that procedures can be incorporated into the programs that will give the user some explanation of the line of reasoning. Because the program has the knowledge available in a form that in some way resembles that of a human expert—for example: "if the patient has a high temperature

and weak legs, influenza is likely"—it can easily be made to display the successive inferences it has made in the process of reaching its conclusions. This is a most important feature, even if the type of explanation given is not very deep, because it enables the users to assess their confidence (or lack of confidence) in the program, the machine seeming no longer a "black box" as it too often does with more ordinary programs.

3. The users. Expert systems must be constructed with a number of practical considerations in mind. First of all, they must be designed to help the non-expert who is looking for advice in some specialized field. The commonest example at present is the doctor in general practice seeking expert advice on renal infections or hypertension before sending his/her patient to see a specialist. This is of particular importance to the country doctor who may be many miles away from the nearest specialist. Thus the systems' level of performance must be comparable with that of human experts in the same field; the program could therefore benefit from the constructive criticism of a possibly changing panel of specialists. An expert system can, and even should, embody the experience of several experts, experience that is not always reported in the standard literature of the subject.

A second type of potential user is anyone who wishes to acquire a professional knowledge of some special subject, which could be provided by an expert system having some instructional features; this aspect is considered in Chapter 18 on Computer Assisted Instruction (CAI). Finally, expert systems can preserve the unique expertise of great specialists, something that is often lost because they retire without handing it on to their successors.

4. Different types of knowledge. The problem of knowledge representation in an expert system is clearly fundamental. Only rarely can the knowledge concerning a particular field be put in terms of a single formalism. There are usually *some items of a heuristic nature* such as "if A and B have been observed then C is plausible but certainly not D", possibly with weights attached to the various conclusions. There are *procedural items* such as "if A is known consider first B and then C, otherwise first C and then B", a type often called "meta-knowledge". A third type is *factual knowledge* such as "A consists of B, C and D". The two first types are usually expressed in the form of production rules in today's expert systems, whilst the third can be expressed more naturally and more economically as a tree structure. Figure 15.2 illustrates this distinction. There is usually great variation among experts where items of the first two types are concerned but a much greater likelihood of agreement over the third: thus the statement "Great Britain consists of England, Scotland and Wales" is one which would be agreed by any geographer. (Figure 15.3).

A distinction can be made between a *knowledge base* and a *data base,* the essential difference being that heuristic items, often included in the former,

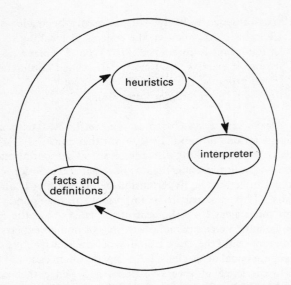

Figure 15.2   Distinction between components of knowledge base

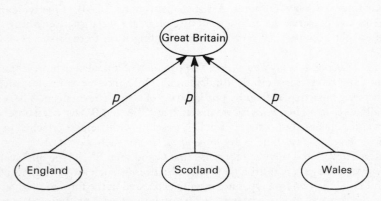

Figure 15.3   Organizational tree for a set of facts (p = "is part of")

are usually absent from, or present only to a very limited extent in, the latter. The facts and definitions included in a knowledge base would be called "data" in a data base; in an expert system the term "data" means those items that relate specifically to the problem being dealt with at the time, and are external to the system proper.

A short guide to the construction of expert systems

Constructing an expert system is an informal activity, more of an art than an exact science. Experience has from time to time suggested a number of principles, which are still rather simple-minded and may sometimes seem to be self-evident. The advice that follows is addressed mainly to the information scientist (IS) who is engaged in developing an expert system in collaboration with an expert in that domain (DE).

(a) Some problems are well adapted to solution by expert systems; these have been classified by Buchanan and Duda[6] and can be described by a variety of terms:
   — Interpretation and/or understanding of a complex mass of data
   — Classification
   — Evaluation of situations
   — Diagnosis—e.g., medical, breakdown of machinery
   — Detection of anomalies in some system, e.g., a circuit
   — crisis management.
   The common feature here is that all such problems involve a large number of heterogeneous and interdependent parameters whose observed values are subject to error and for which there are not standard interpretations.

(b) It is essential that a genuine expert is available throughout the whole period of the project, and that several other experts can be called upon to criticize and improve the prototype version. The strength of a human expert, in medicine for example, lies not in an encyclopedic knowledge of diseases (which can be got from a book), but rather in the ability to develop strategies and to know the "tricks of the trade" which he uses to arrive swiftly and surely at the correct diagnosis: these "tricks" are the fruit of long experience and are seldom to be found in books. It is of prime importance to include all the unusual—often serious—cases met by the expert. An experienced specialist will often go straight to the heart of a problem because he/she know what are the right questions to ask: these are not necessarily the standard ones, but are suggested by signs that he/she can recognize.

(c) There is the question of the level of the knowledge used. In the present state of the art it is important to include only information that has a sufficiently sound technical basis, in other words not to include too much that is derived from "commonsense" or "everyday life". A medical diagnosis program can take into account such parameters as the patient's nervous state or tendency to alcoholism; but it is not necessary to include such statements as "coffee is bad for the nerves", or, still worse, "arabica has less caffeine than robusta". The nth generation of expert systems

($n > 5$) may perhaps integrate such information into their knowledge bases.

(d) *Building the first version.* At the start the information scientist (IS) must become familiar with the vocabulary of the domain expert (DE) so that he can record the procedures given by DE for solving typical cases. This will give IS an idea of the essential parameters for the domain, the intermediate steps in the reasoning and the preliminary strategies used in tackling a problem. It will also show IS how a consultation is normally conducted and what is the normal order in which data are acquired. Thus a medical consultation may consist of these episodes:

— basic data for the patient (age, sex, . . .)
— what is the trouble?
— what observations does the doctor make?
— what is the patient's medical history?
— results of any previous examinations?
— provisional diagnosis
— suggestions for further examinations or tests
— recommendations of treatment

(e) *Extending the first version.* This first version will soon achieve good performance with the typical cases on which its construction has been based, but shortcomings in the reasoning mechanisms will be revealed when it is applied to real-life problems more varied than the first. It may prove necessary to make some significant changes in the organization of the program in going from the first version to a second version that will show a closer approach to "expert" behavior.

The first version can be regarded as a feasibility study, to show that a program can actually be written that makes use of a large body of knowledge in a particular field in order to achieve a certain aim. Once the prototype has been made to work it can be demonstrated on a range of problems; the next requirement is to make its use "natural" and "friendly". Here "natural" means that the dialog between the user and the program is conducted along the normal lines of human dialog, for example with the program putting questions in an order that does not seem disconcerting to the user. In this connection it is useful to recall that a human expert will often ask questions that do not bear directly on the solution to the problem under discussion but form part of the method of communicating information or of acquiring more information; the program can behave similarly. "Friendly" means that the questions (put by either side) should be clear and in a form as close as possible to natural language, with possibilities for explanations or supplementary questions to make their meaning clearer; and responses by the program should be in clear, not in code or too condensed. The user should not have to bother with technical details concerning the use of the console, such as having to end every line with some special symbol when his input overruns one or more lines: he/she is not required to be a computer expert, and all such matters should be dealt with by the interface modules.

The system should be able to give explanations for its behavior, at two levels. It should be able to explain why it is asking a question, and thus to show the user what it is trying to do; and it should be able to explain how it has arrived at its conclusion, in other words to trace its reasoning path. Both these abilities are of major importance in gaining the user's confidence by making it possible for the user to confirm that the program is behaving correctly—or, if need be, to criticize it. Some sophisticated systems provide for the recording of complaints, to be studied later by the designers; these can range from suggestions for ways in which the user interface could be improved to criticisms of some of the rules used by the system, possibly backed up by counter-examples. Finally, every expert system should be able to keep a record of the problems put to it, for reasons both of providing statistics of its use and of suggesting improvements. Whenever new rules are added to the system, tests should be made to check that problems that were handled satisfactorily before the change are still so handled.

(f) *Keeping the expert's interest.* AI suffered for a long time from the predictions of enthusiastic practitioners who made extravagent claims about what the computer would be able to do before too long. The consequent scepticism must be overcome by developing quickly a prototype and showing that it actually works, even if its achievements are not quite up to the original aim. The expert who was involved in the construction of the system will be encouraged to continue if he/she soon sees some of his/her own reasoning processes represented in the machine. At the same time, it is important that purely technical problems concerning operating systems, programming languages and so on are kept away from the expert: there is no call for him/her to become a computer scientist, just as there is no call for the computer scientist to become an expert in this particular field. Above all, the expert should never be criticized for any apparent lack of logic in his reasoning processes; such a lack is often inherent in the nature of the field, but also it is often more apparent than real since it may hide implicit steps in the reasoning that the expert has not revealed.

(g) *Evaluating the program.* This can be done from several points of view, and that of the information scientist, whose aim may be to show that his method is twice as fast as that used on other systems, may conflict with that of the future users who may have quite different criteria. Even if it turns out that the performance compares well with that of other systems, there is the danger of raising comparisons with human experts. Another risk is that users who are not information scientists may criticize the system for not being sufficiently easy to use. In the case of the MYCIN program for diagnosing blood infections, only 75% of its first results were confirmed by experts in the field, which was disappointing; but later comparisons made by V. L. Yu,[7] concerning meningitis, showed that there was no better agreement when the diagnoses made by one set of experts were reviewed by others: the apparently poor performance, therefore, was the consequence of a lack of consensus among experts rather than any failing in the program.

Comparing the program with human experts is generally a more complicated matter than a simple count of percentage success, for several reasons. First, cases must be found for which the correct result is known, or failing that, for which there is consensus among experts; thus in the case of possible accidents in a nuclear power station, all that can be done is to simulate incidents for which there are already records. Then the system may have an advantage resulting from its restriction to one particular field, and this is difficult to assess; a human expert may have a broader field of knowledge and be led to form hypotheses that lie outside the particular field under consideration, and thus to follow a wrong track before seeing which is the right one. From this point of view, therefore, the human expert can be at a disadvantage.

Finally, a further source of difficulty in providing objective comparisons is that present-day systems, lacking any connection with means for perception such as a camera, cannot see, in the physical sense of the word; they have to be given their data by a human intermediary who may not give an objective description, and who may interpose a certain amount of interpretation. A human expert put in the same situation could be rather thrown off course because he/she was working in unfamiliar conditions.

Expert systems and transfer of expertise

The fields in which expert systems are valuable are those for which the solution space is so large that it is necessary to seek the help of a human expert, who will make his/her knowledge and experience available in the course of a number of sessions with the information scientist. It has been found possible in a few simple cases to construct a system from examples for which the solution is already known—see Chapter 19; but in most cases it will be necessary to question human experts about their way of working, the strategies which they use and the "tricks" which they have acquired gradually in the course of experience, and of which they are often not consciously aware. This will generally take place in two stages: first the transfer of knowledge from the domain expert (DE) to the information scientist (IS) and then from the information scientist to the program to be developed (see Fig. 15.4).

DE will often forget items of knowledge or omit steps in his/her

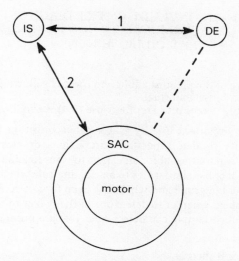

Figure 15.4 Classical schema for the transfer of expertise

reasoning, as will be discovered gradually by IS, and DE will also give incorrect rules that have to be corrected later. A checking program—usually called a data-acquisition program—is invaluable, because it enables faults in the knowledge base to be picked up immediately, before even starting to test the program. Various software tools have been developed for this purpose and are incorporated into some programs.

One way to simplify checking the knowledge base is to use a clear formalism that removes any need to master some particular programming language. Thus in ROSIE[8] for example a rule can be expressed in phrases that resemble natural language; in the following the keywords are in capitals:

if:	THERE IS	an operating system
	WHOSE	host computer IS KNOWN
	AND WHOSE	prompt-character IS KNOWN
	AND WHOSE	type IS NOT KNOWN
then:	DEDUCE	the type OF the operating system
	AND SEND	concat ("this is a" the type of the operating system "system")
	TO	user

Another method is to generate natural-language statements of the rules from their internal representation, thus making them comprehensible generally, and in particular to the domain expert who is seldom an information scientist. Thus for EMYCIN[9] a rule recorded in LISP

PREMISE:($AND (SAME CNTXT AGE ADULT)
              (SAME CNTXT LEAVES—YELLOWING)
              (SAME CNTXT STEM—COLOR—ABNORMAL))

ACTION: (CONCLUDE CNTXT DIAGNOSTIC TALLY
                '((FUSARIOSE 400
                (VERTICILLIOSE 400)))

is translated as

if: the age of the plant is: adult, and there is yellowing of leaves and if
       stem color is abnormal
then: possible diagnostics are: fusariose (0.4) verticilliose (0.4)

Another very important quality that a data-acquisition program should
have is the ability to detect possible interactions or even contradictions
between rules. It is not unusual for an expert to want to add a new rule to the
system, which in fact has similarities to an existing rule which may have been
in the system for a long time and which has been forgotten. A quick decision
may have to be taken, whether to delete one of the two or to replace both by a
third. EMYCIN for example can detect rules that are not independent, such
as:

R1:   if   A & B then X
R2:   if   A & B & C then Y

Whenever R2 is activated so too is R1 and this is, in effect, a message from the
program to the (human) user who is invited to think over the problem.

Metaknowledge

The name means "knowledge about knowledge", a kind of second-level
knowledge that maps on to first-level knowledge. The distinction between the
two levels is not always very clear, so much so that the difficulty of
representing metaknowledge has led many workers to use the same representation for this as for other types. One person's metaknowledge may in fact be
another's knowledge.

Thus the concept of metaknowledge is a relative one and the number of
levels is arbitrary; if there is a highest meta-level for a system this will be
something like the "awareness" it has of its own knowledge.

Consider the following rules:

M1:   When several inferences can be drawn take first the one most rec-
      ently provided
M2:   The program knows nothing about botany
M3:   If it is winter first try those rules that diagnose influenza.

Few programs contain knowledge of the type of M1, because the date of a
rule is usually either not recorded or is incorporated into the interpreter.

Neither are items like M2 generally recorded; the designers of a program prefer to limit themselves to giving positive rather than negative knowledge—and a list of things the program does not know would, by definition, be infinite. Finally, a rule of the type of M3 could be included in a medical diagnosis system on the same level as "if the patient is shivering, consider influenza"; but it is different in that it does not give the conclusion "influenza" as a medical rule does but simply suggests an order in which the rules should be applied. It is thus at a more general level than the medical knowledge itself.

It is usual today to regard the knowledge provided by the expert as occupying three levels: factual knowledge, heuristics and metaknowledge.[10] Each level is illustrated in this example from petroleum geology:

Factual: Carboniferous preceded Permian
Heuristic: If a zone is found to contain graptoliths it is probably
                    Silurian or Ordovician
Metaknowledge: Study the wireline logs before the analysis of the cores.

The first is a statement of fact accepted by all geologists. The second is a rule for reasoning that also would have the support of the specialists, but which nevertheless is inductive in nature and could be modified if a geologist found graptoliths in a zone of another period. The third is a rule of behavior whose result is advice concerning the order in which certain items of information should be used; it could vary from one geologist to another, depending on the relative availability of different sources of information.

The problems in developing very large systems, possibly with thousands of rules, make it essential to be able to represent knowledge on several different levels.

Tools and formalisms for expert systems

There are several languages that can be used to express the knowledge base of an expert system,* often relating to one particular system from which the part independent of the domain has been extracted. Table 15.1 lists these in three categories according to the type of logic used.

---

* To my knowledge, PLANNER and FOL have not been used to develop expert systems.

Table 15.1 Programming languages related to expert systems, grouped according to logical bases. Reference (superior figures) on pages 156-157.

1. First-order predicate logic:

Language	Author(s)	Place
PLANNER	Hewitt[11]	MIT
PROLOG	Roussel[12]	Marseille
	Colmerauer[13]	Marseille
	Warren[14]	Edinburgh
SNARK	Laurière[15]	Paris VI
FOL	Weyhrauch[16]	Stanford
TANGO	Cordier[31]	Orsay

2. Production rules:

EMYCIN	Van Melle[9]	Stanford
OPS	Forgy[17]	Carnegie-Mellon
EXPERT	Weiss[18]	Rutgers
KAS	Reboh[19]	SRI International
RAINBOW	Hollander[20]	IBM Palo Alto
ARGOS-II	Farreny[21]	Toulouse

3. Semantic networks, objects:

KRL	Bobrow, Winograd[22]	Xerox PARC
OWL	Szolovits[23]	MIT
UNITS	Stefik[24]	Stanford
FRL	Roberts[25]	MIT
AIMDS	Sridharan[26]	Rutgers
KLONE	Brachman[27]	BBN
ORBIT	Steels[28]	Schlumberger
HPRL	Rosenberg[29]	Hewlett-Packard
LOOPS	Bobrow, Stefik[32]	Xerox PARC
KEE	Kehler[33]	IntelliCorp

Limitations of present expert systems

Systems are too superficial. The main limitation of the expert systems that exist today derives from their lack of representation of the deep structure of the relations they are able to make between different phenomena. A program such as MYCIN is very powerful when it is a question of associating symptoms and diagnoses, interpreting observations on bacterial cultures, etc., but contains no model of the composition of the blood or of the mechanism of coagulation, nor any knowledge at all of the role of the heart in the circulatory system. So long as all goes well with the use of the system the lack of such deep structure knowledge does not prevent it from reaching the correct diagnosis; but it can prove a serious limitation if conflicts arise between hypotheses—and it is here that the human expert shows his superiority. Such a conflict cannot be resolved by some simple manipulation of plausibilities but requires a deeper study of the causes of the phenomena observed.

Rapid degradation of performance. This occurs when the problem posed falls outside the program's domain of competence, which is often narrow; and this results also from the inability of the system to use "commonsense" to infer missing data. Humans have more general reasoning powers and a deeper understanding of problems, which enable them to deal with such situations even though their performance declines, though more gradually, in the two cases.

Interfaces that are still crude. The subtle problem of understanding natural language can still be a source of difficulty for the user. However, it is likely that this situation will be improved in the near future as a result of the progress that has been made in developing natural-language interfaces to databases.

Difficulty of modifying the strategy. It has already been said that the strategies used by the interpreters of the knowledge base are usually programmed: that is, they are procedural in nature. But some part of the expertise resides in these strategies and it would therefore be preferable to have them represented by production rules so as to make modification and development easier. The use of meta-rules in the TIRESIAS[30] system is a step in this direction and should be followed up.

Reasoning is not of only one type. An important contribution to the power of human reasoning is made by the extraordinary ability to adapt to the prevailing situation and to use different strategies according to that situation. Expert systems based on production rules or other standard methods are incapable of short-circuiting their normal procedures in special cases. Some human experts can at times take instant decisions simply because something in the situation they are confronted with reminds them of something they have met in the past and they have no need to go through the processes of formulating and testing hypotheses as they would normally do.

The two following chapters give several examples of expert systems developed for industrial and medical applications.

Notes and references

[1] General methods for reasoning depend fundamentally on conceptualizations at a higher level than the particular problem to be solved.

[2] McCorduck, P. (1979), *Machines who think*, Freeman, San Francisco. This book traces the history of artificial intelligence, and in particular gives the origins of the DENDRAL project.

[3] Feigenbaum E. A., Buchanan B. G., Lederberg J. (1971), "On generality and problem solving: a case study using the DENDRAL program." *Machine Intelligence*, Vol. 6, Meltzer & Michie (eds.), New York, Elsevier, New York, pp. 165-190.

[4] Kuhn T. (1970), *The structure of scientific revolutions*, 2nd edition, Chicago, University of Chicago.

[5] Barstow D., Buchanan B. G. (1981), "Maxims for knowledge engineering", *Stanford University memo*, HPP-81-4.

[6] Buchanan B. G., Duda R. (1982), "Principles of rule-based expert systems", *Stanford University memo*, HPP-82-14.

[7] Yu V. L., Fagan L. M. et al. (1979), "Antimicrobial selection by a computer: a blinded evaluation by infectious disease experts", *J. Amer. Med. Assoc.* 241-12, pp. 1279-1282.

[8] Fain J., Hayes-Roth F., Sowizral H., Waterman D. (1981), "Programming Examples in ROSIE, Rand Corporation", *Technical Report*, N-1646-ARPA.

[9] Van Melle W. (1980), "A domain-independent system that aids in constructing knowledge-based consultation programs", *PhD Dissertation*, Stanford Univ. Computer Science Department, STAN-CS-80-820.

[10] Hayes-Roth F., Waterman D. A., Lenat D. B. (eds.) (1983), *Building expert systems*, Reading, Mass., Addison-Wesley.

[11] Hewitt C. (1972), "Description and theoretical analysis (using schemata) of PLANNER: a language for proving theorems and manipulating models in a robot", *PhD Thesis*, Department of Mathematics, MIT.

[12] Roussel P. (1975), *PROLOG, Manuel de référence et d'utilisation*, Marseille, Groupe d'Intelligence Artificielle, U.E.R. de Luminy, Université d'Aix-Marseille.

[13] Colmerauer A., Kanoui H., Van Caneghem M. (1983), "Prolog, bases théoriques et développements actuels", *RAIRO/TSI*, Vol. 2 n°4, pp. 271-311.

[14] Warren D., et al. (1977), "PROLOG: The language and its implementation compared with LISP", *Proc. SIGART/SIPLAN Symposium on Programming Languages*, Rochester, N.Y.

[15] Laurière J. L., *Introduction à l'intelligence artificielle* (in preparation).

[16] Weyhrauch R. W. (1980), "Prolegomena to a theory of mechanized formal reasoning", *Artificial Intelligence*, 13, 1-2, April 1980.

[17] Forgy C., McDermott J. (1977), "OPS, a domain-independent production system language", *Proc. IJCAI-77*, pp. 953-939.

[18] Weiss S., Kulikowski C. (1979), "EXPERT: A system for developing consultation models", *Proc. IJCAI-79*, pp. 942-947.

[19] Reboh R. (1981), "Knowledge engineering techniques and tools in the prospector environment", *Tech. Note 243*, Artificial Intelligence Center, SRI International, Menlo Park, Cal., June 1981.

[20] Hollander C. R., Reinstein H. C. (1979), "A knowledge-based application definition system", *Proc. IJCAI-79*, pp. 397-399.

[21] Farreny H. (1981), "Un système de maintenance automatique d'inter-relations dans un système de production", *Congrès de reconnaissance des formes et intelligence artificelle*, Nancy, pp. 751-761.

[22] Bobrow D., Winograd T. (1977), "An overview of KRL, a knowledge representation language", *Cognitive Science* 1, 1, pp. 3-46.

[23] Szolovits P., Pauker S. G. (1978), "Categorical and probabilistic reasoning in medical diagnosis", *Artificial Intelligence* 11, pp. 115-144.

[24] Stefik M. (1979), "An examination of a frame-structured representation system", *Proc. IJCAI-79*, pp. 845-852.

[25] Roberts R. B., Goldstein I. P. (1977), "The FRL primer", *MIT AI Lab Memo 408*.

[26] Sridharan N. S. (1980), "Representational facilities of AIMDS: a sampling", *Tech. Report No. CBM-TM-86*, Dept. of Computer Science, Rutgers Univ.

[27] Brachman R. J. (1977), "What's in a concept: structural foundations for semantic networks", *Int. Jnl Man-Machine Studies* 9, p. 127-152.

[28] Steels L. (1982), "An applicative view of object-oriented programming", *European Conference on Integrated Interactive Computing Systems*, Stresa, Italy.

[29] Rosenberg S. (1983), "HPRL: a language for building expert systems", *IJCAI-83*, Karlsruhe, August 1983, pp. 215-217.

[30] Davis R. (1977), "Knowledge acquisition in rule-based systems: knowledge about representation or a basis for system construction and maintenance", in *Pattern-directed inference systems*, Waterman Hayes-Roth (eds.).

[31] Cordier M. O., Rousset M. C. (1984), "TANGO: moteur d'inférences pour un système expert avec variables", *4e Congrès de Reconnaissance des formes et intelligence artificielle*, Paris.

[32] Bobrow D. G., Stefik M. (1983), *The LOOPS manual*, Xerox PARC, Palo Alto.

[33] Kehler T. P., Clemenson C. D. (1984), "An application system for expert systems", *Systems and Software*, pp. 212-224.

16
Expert Systems in Medicine and Biology

Introduction

Medicine has been a favorite field for development of expert systems, and for this reason has been given a chapter to itself. One of the first applications of computers in medicine was to patients' records, with the dual aims of improving administration and gathering more information on illnesses.[1] Medical histories often provide the material for databases from which statistical conclusions can be drawn, such as the probability that a man of under 40 will recover from a stomach cancer within five years.

More recently, the problem of assisting medical diagnosis has been tackled, either by using the databases already available to deduce important relations between symptoms and diagnoses, by applying various algorithmic or mathematical methods or, most recently, by using techniques derived from artificial intelligence, such as expert systems. Brief descriptions of the first two types of method are given in this chapter and their limitations indicated, so as to show the importance of the later methods depending on expert systems.

There are several reasons why doctors and information scientists have been collaborating for many years. An important one is that many reports[2] have shown that errors in diagnosis and in prescribing antibiotics are common, with consequent high costs to society in both clinical and economic terms. The idea arose fairly soon that the computer would not suffer from human weaknesses such as forgetfulness due to fatigue, or failure to consider the possibility of a certain diagnosis, and might therefore perform better in matters involving interpretation of technical data where the doctor's personal attention is of less importance. The first essays in this direction used statistical and algorithmic methods, which were the only ones available in the 1960s; but the limitations of these soon became evident.

Mathematical methods

Classification techniques have been used to determine the most likely diagnosis from a set of observations.[4] A discrimination function enables objects to be classified according to the presence or absence of certain signs or symptoms. The method consists of choosing a set of objects (here, the patients) for which the distribution among the classes is known; a class can be described by a vector $X = (x_1, \ldots x_n)$ where the x_j are the characteristic parameters and the discriminating function has the form

$$P\,(D/X) = \sum_{j=1}^{n} a_j x_j$$

where the a_j are derived from a study of a large number of patients. The function is computed for each new patient to decide whether or not he belongs to a class already known—in other words, whether or not the diagnosis matches his case well enough. The difficulty with this method is that of getting a sufficiently reliable sample of patients from which to determine values of the a_j that genuinely characterize the illness.

Another simple algorithmic method is to use decision trees; each node corresponds to a question and the reply leads to another node, and so on until a leaf of the tree is reached, giving the diagnosis. This has the advantage from the point of view of information science of being simple to put into operation but suffers from two serious disadvantages: the possibility that the subject may not be able to reply to a question must be provided for explicitly (otherwise it may block the process) and it is very difficult to modify the tree, should better clinical knowledge become available or a mistake be discovered.

The Bayesian method[5,6] allows the probability that a patient is suffering from a particular illness to be calculated from observations of the patient together with a knowledge of the relative frequency with which the different symptoms occur in each given condition. If $P\,(S/M_i)$ is the probability of observing the symptom (or group of symptoms) S in a patient suffering from illness M_i and $P\,(M_i)$ the a priori probability of M_i in the population concerned, then if S is observed in an individual patient the probability that he is suffering from M_i is:

$$P\,(M_i/S) = \frac{P\,(M_i)\ P\,(S/M_i)}{\displaystyle\sum_{i=1}^{n} P\,(M_i)\ P\,(S/M_i)}$$

The Bayesian method has limitations in the medical field for these reasons:

(1). The elements of the very large array of conditional probabilities entering into the expression on the right are seldom known with any accuracy; the need to use default values for missing data reduces the accuracy of the result.

(2). Strictly, the rule assumes that the illnesses are mutually exclusive and that all possibilities are taken into account—conditions that rarely hold in practice.

(3). It is difficult to justify the decision if challenged, other than by displaying the complete array giving the corelations between symptoms and diagnoses: a criticism that clearly applies to any method based on statistical techniques.

Bayesian medical diagnosis in action is shown in Fig. 16.1; but we can take it for granted that this is not the way doctors work.

$$P(M_i/S) = \frac{P(M_i)\,P(S/M_i)}{\sum_{i=1}^{n} P(M_i)\,P(S/M_i)}$$

Figure 16.1   Medical diagnosis by the Bayesian method

Methods that are intermediate between mathematics and AI

Database analysis can be used to complement methods based on expert-system techniques to predict the course of an illness or to recommend treatment; such a method will use records taken over a period of time, and for a number of patients, of the values of the clinical parameters that are considered to be significant, rather than inference and deduction rules provided by practitioners. An example is the ARAMIS[7] project of John Fries at Stanford. Whenever a new patient is examined the doctor selects a number of indices with which to enter the database in order to find a similar patient or group of patients for whom the treatment and progress of the illness have been recorded, thus suggesting to him a possible treatment for his present patient.

This method provides a semi-automatic reasoning process using the analogy of the database, and its success depends on making the right choice of parameters with which to search this. Several attempts have been made, for example by Robert Blum,[8] to devise rules to guide this choice, depending on a statistical analysis of the base, but here there is a risk of serious loss of reliability because of missing or erroneous data. Mistakes arising in this way no longer occur when the information is used as an expert system because an experienced doctor will have long since eliminated any contradictions he may have met, using his own reasoning powers to arrive at the correct general rules. However, statistical analysis can provide valuable indications of correlations, notably the weights used in "fuzzy reasoning" by human experts, which can be used in the rules incorporated into expert systems.

Expert systems

The great novelty here is that there is no requirement to decide in advance how the knowledge contained in the system is to be used; which is in complete contradiction to the traditional programming methods.

The most famous systems, all written after 1973, are MYCIN,[9] PIP,[10] INTERNIST/CADUCEUS,[11] VM,[12] CASNET/EXPERT[13,14]; there are also PUFF,[15] IRIS,[16] using different methods. The differences between these systems lie in the different formalisms they use to represent their knowledge, such as production rules, semantic networks, "frames", and in the different measures they use for the strength of association between signs or symptoms on the one hand and diagnoses on the other. There are also differences between the strategies they employ: some try to achieve a diagnosis whose likelihood exceeds a given threshold value, others to increase the difference between possible diagnoses, using mainly differential-diagnosis strategies for this purpose. Finally, they differ in their capacity for explaining and justifying their actions, a property that is essential for the gaining of the confidence of the doctors, both those who are involved in the development of the system and those who will use it.

The following sections describe the main medically-oriented systems.

MYCIN

The aim of this system is to diagnose infectious illnesses, especially infections of the blood and of the cerebro-spinal (meningeal) fluid; it attempts to identify the bacteria responsible for the patient's illness and hence to suggest a therapy, together with the dose required. The standard situation is that a patient shows signs of infection, a sample of blood or urine is taken and cultures grown from this; the information so gained is expressed in the form of production rules (see Chapter 12) associated with a number of contexts and the contexts are arranged hierarchically in a tree structure, an example of which is shown in Fig. 16.2. This example relates to a patient from whom three cultures have been grown (two recent, one old) and on whom one operation has been performed; an organism has been isolated in each of the two recent cultures, but the patient is under treatment (with two medicaments) for only one of these; two have been isolated in the older culture and treatment, with one medicament, has been given for one of these. This tree of contexts is valuable not only because it gives a structure to the clinical problem but also it enables reference to be made to different occurences of the same concept, thus acting as a variable in the mathematical sense of the term.

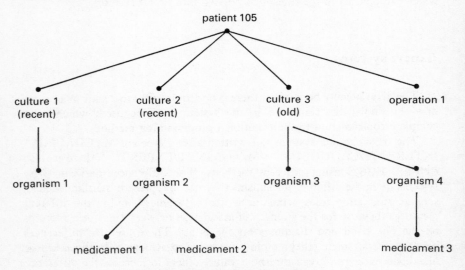

Figure 16.2   MYCIN context tree

The rules used by the program are easily shown in a form resembling natural language. Thus if one types PR 37, meaning Print Rule 37, MYCIN responds

Rule 37   if: 1. the identity of the germ is not known with certainty and
            2. the germ is Gram-negative and
            3. the morphology of the organism is "rod" and
            4. the germ is aerobic
        then: there is a strong probability (0.8) that the germ is of the type "enterobacteriacae".

This example shows that MYCIN computes coefficients to indicate the strength of its conclusions; these are combined in the way explained in Chapter 12 in the discussion of uncertain ("fuzzy") reasoning.

MYCIN was a pioneer among systems developed to aid medical diagnosis. Although it has not been used in hospitals it has had a strong influence on all research into methods for representing the reasoning processes of experts in different subjects, even outside the medical field. The acceptance of the need to separate the knowledge base from the interpreter owes much to what was done in MYCIN; the system has also been used in a teaching role, to demostrate its reasoning methods to medical students.

PIP (Present Illness Program)

This was developed at MIT to diagnose kidney disorders. The medical knowledge here is put in the form of hierarchical objects (see Chapter 13), of which an example, for acute glomerulonephritis, is given in Fig. 16.3. An object can have several types of attribute; some bring the object into active consideration (it becomes ACTIVE), others suggest that it might be considered (it becomes SEMI-ACTIVE), yet others cause it to be discarded (it becomes INACTIVE). In the manipulation of the objects an active object is always tested and attention transferred to the best semi-active candidate if the active object ceases to be such. It can happen that the state of one object is changed during the testing of another, either because the two are mutually exclusive, because they are in competition, or because they are complementary.

trigger:	edema with location=facial or periorbital
	not painful
	not asymmetric
	not erythematous
confirmed by:	weakness, anorexia
caused by:	streptococcal infection – recent
causes:	sodium retention, hypertension, nephrotic syndrome, glomerulitis
complicated by:	acute renal failure
complications:	cellulitis
differential diagnosis:	chronic hypertension implies acute glomerulitis
	repeated edema implies nephrotic syndrome
	abdominal pain implies Henoch-Schonlein purpura

Figure 16.3   Part of the object "Acute glomerulonephritis" in PIP

INTERNIST/CADUCEUS

This was developed at the Universty of Pittsburgh; it incorporates information on about 350 diagnoses in internal medicine taking into account about 5000 symptoms and signs.

The knowledge base of the system is represented in the form of a taxonomic structure of illnesses. There are links in two directions between illnesses and observations, the latter comprising symptoms, signs and clinical data, and each link is assigned a measure of strength. One direction is expressed by OBSERVATION SUGGESTS DIAGNOSIS and has a strength between 0 and 5; the other is DIAGNOSIS PRESUMES OBSERVATION and has a strength between 1 and 5, representing the frequency with which a certain observation is associated with a particular illness.

The control structure of INTERNIST/CADUCEUS is unusual in that it depends primarily on differential diagnosis: two hypotheses are said to be in competition if the combination of the two, regarded as a single hypothesis, explains no more observations than either taken alone. There are three strategic principles, as follows.

(1). ELIMINATION: if more than four hypotheses are in competition look for NEGATIVE OBSERVATIONS that will enable the number of competitors to be reduced.
(2). DISCRIMINATION: if between two and four hypotheses are in competition, concentrate on the top pair and look for more information so as to give them different scores.
(3). PURSUIT: if all but two diagnoses have been eliminated look for information that will take the difference between their scores above some given threshold.

VM (Ventilator Manager)

This was developed by Larry Fagan[12] as part of a collaborative project between Stanford and a San Francisco hospital. Its aim is to interpret real-time quantitative observations made on patients in an intensive care unit; it undertakes the following tasks:

(a) detecting possible errors in the measurements;
(b) recognizing that in some way all is not as it should be with the life-support system and suggesting action to be taken;
(c) summarizing the patient's physiological state;
(d) suggesting changes in the treatment, taking into account the way the patient's state is changing and the long-term aims of the treatment, such as that he will be able to breathe naturally again;
(e) predicting the normal response to the treatment so as to check that it is proceeding satisfactorily.

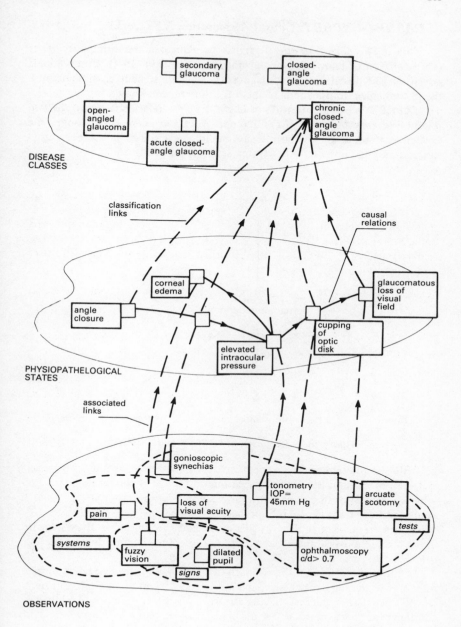

Figure 16.4 Three-level description of an illness (*after Weiss*[13])

CASNET-EXPERT (Causal ASsociation NETwork)

This is specialized to the diagnosis of glaucoma. Its originality is its representation of knowledge on several levels (see Fig. 16.4)—observations, physio–pathological states and diagnoses, a separation made possible because the physiological implications of the infection are well known.

EXPERT is a generalization of CASNET, the relation between the two resembling that between EMYCIN and MYCIN; there is no longer the explicit representation of the physio–pathological states. It has been used subsequently to construct other systems, as shown in Fig.16.5.

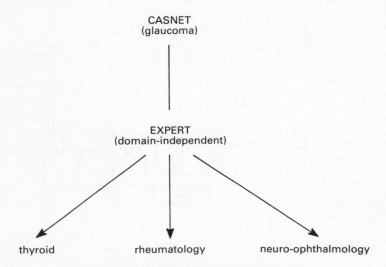

Figure 16.5 Evolution of CASNET and EXPERT

EXPERT's rules are of three types:
- — associations between observations
- — associations between observations and hypotheses
- — associations between hypotheses

The rules are always applied in this order and the linking is always in the forward direction—compare the working of inference engines for production rules, discussed in Chapter 12.

In contrast to MYCIN the strength of a link is not increased when several rules lead to the same conclusion; instead the coefficient of maximum value is taken. Thus if an hypothesis having already a plausibility value of 0.6 receives additional support of value 0.4 its plausibility remains at 0.6, whereas in MYCIN this would become $0.6 + 0.4 - 0.24 = 0.76$. The results, however, are not very different, because the likelihood or plausibility coefficients have different meanings in the two systems and are used differently in the two:

whilst MYCIN awards the extra weight EXPERT takes what may be called the intrinsic weight but at the end of the calculation awards a special bonus to the hypothesis that is supported by the greatest number of rules—which suggests that it is the most consistent hypothesis.

The fact that EXPERT is written in FORTRAN means that it is easily transportable; but the large number of abbreviations used make it very difficult to read.

Table 16.1 summarizes the main expert systems developed for medical application.

Theme	Name	Author
Blood infections and Meningitis	MYCIN	Shortliffe[9]
Internal medicine	INTERNIST/CADUCEUS	Pople[11]
Cancer	ONCOCIN	Shortliffe[18]
Glaucoma	CASNET	Weiss[13]
Renal disorders	PIP	Pauker[10]
Monitoring patients in intensive care	VM	Fagan[12]
Pulmonary infections	PUFF	Kunz[15]
Epigastric pains	SPHINX	Fieschi[19]
Ophthalmology	IRIS	Trigoboff[16]
Cardiology	DIGITALIS	Gorry[20]
pH control	ABEL	Patil[21]
Planning biological experiments	MOLGEN	Martin[22]
Protein analysis	CRYSALIS	Engelmore[23]
Arterial hypertension	SAM	Gascuel[24]

Table 16.1 Expert systems for medicine

The state of the art

In spite of the lack of depth—at the physiological level for example—in the associations between phenomena that expert systems can establish, these systems already have a diagnostic power that could be valuable in a hospital. The unwillingness of many doctors to make use of what they regard as a machine's reasoning is still to be overcome but the possibility of easily following the route by which the program has reached its conclusions, and checking the rules it has used, should be a valuable help in this. What must be done soon is to transfer these expert systems to small computers that can be used by the doctor in his own surgery, so that there is no longer any need to use a telecommunication link to access a big program running on a distant machine. It must also be made possible for the doctors themselves to modify the programs without always having to call in a computer scientist to help; and this implies an improvement in the interface between the user and the machine.

Notes and references

[1] Degoulet P., Chantalou J.-P., Chatelier G., Devriès C., Goupy S., Zweigenbaum P. (1983), "Structured and standardized medical records", Van Demmel, Ball and Wigertz (eds.), *MEDINFO-83*, New York, North-Holland, pp. 1164-1168.

[2] Ledley R., Lusted L. (1959), "Reasoning foundations of medical diagnosis", *Science*, 130, pp. 9-21.

[3] Junin C. M., Tupasu T., Craig W. A. (1973), "Use of antibiotics, a brief exposition of the problem and some tentative solutions", *Anns. Int. Medicine*, 79, pp. 555-560.

[4] Duda R. O., Hart P. E. (1973), *Pattern classification and scene analysis*, New York, Wiley.

[5] Lusted L. B. (1968), *Introduction to medical decision making*, Springfield, Ill., Charles C. Thomas.

[6] De Dombal F. T., Gremy F. (eds.) (1976), *Decision making and medical care: can information science help?*, New York, North-Holland.

[7] Fries J. F. (1972), "Time-oriented patient records and a computer databank", *J. Amer. Med. Assoc.*, 222, pp. 1536-1542.

[8] Blum R. (1982), "Discovery and representation of causal relationships from a large time-oriented clinical database: the RX project", *Department of Computer Science report*, STAN-CS-82900, Stanford University.

[9] Shortliffe E. H. (1976), *Computer-based medical consultations: MYCIN*, New York, Elsevier.

[10] Pauker S., Gorry A., Kassirer J., Schwartz W. (1976), "Towards the simulation of clinical cognition . . . Taking a present illness by computer", *American Journal of Medicine*, June 1976, 60, pp. 981-996.

[11] Pople H. (1982), "Heuristic methods for imposing structure on ill-structured problems; the structuring of medical diagnostics", in *Artificial Intelligence in medicine*, P. Szolovits (ed.), Boulder, Colorado, Westview Press.

[12] Fagan L. M. (1980), VM "Representing time-dependent relations in a clinical setting", *Ph. D dissertation*, Heuristic Programming Project, Stanford University.

[13] Weiss S., Kulikowski C., Safir A. (1978), "A model-based method for computer-aided medical decision making", *Journal of Artificial Intelligence*, 11, pp. 145-172.

[14] Kulikowski C., Weiss S. (1982), "Representation of expert knowledge for consultation: the CASNET and EXPERT projects", in *Artificial Intelligence in medicine*, P. Szolovits (ed.), Boulder, Colorado, Westview Press.

[15] Kunz et al. (1978), "A physiological rule-based system for interpreting pulmonary function test results", *Heuristic programming project report*, HPP-78-19, Stanford University.

[16] Trigoboff M., Kulilowski C. (1977), "IRIS, A system for the propagation of inferences in a semantic net", *IJCAI-77*, pp. 274-280.

[17] De Dombal F. T., Leaper D. J., Staniland J. R. (1972), Computer-aided diagnosis of acute abdominal pain", *British Medical Journal*, pp. 9-13.

[18] Shortliffe E. H., Scott C. A., Bischoff M. B., Campbell A. B., Van Melle W., Jacobs C. D. (1981), "ONCOCIN; an expert system for oncology protocol management", *IJCAI-81*, pp. 876-881.

[19] Fieschi M. (1981), "Aide à la décision en médicine: le système SPHINX. Application au diagnostic d'une douleur épigastrique". *Thèse de Doctorat en Médecine*, Marseille.

[20] Gorry G. A., Silverman H., Pauker S. G. (1978), "Capturing clinical expertise: a computer program that considers clinical responses to digitalis", *American Journal of Medicine*, pp. 452-460.

[21] Patil R., Szolovits P., Schwartz W. B. (1982), "Modeling knowledge of the patient in acid-base and electrolyte disorders", in *Artificial Intelligence in medicine*, Szolovits (ed.), Boulder, Colorado, Westview Press.

[22] Martin N., Friedland P., King J., Stefik M. (1977), "Knowledge-based management for experiment planning in molecular genetics", *IJCAI-77*, pp. 882-887.

[23] Engelmore R., Terry A. (1979), "Structure and function of the crysalis system", *IJCAI-79*, pp. 250-256.

[24] Gascuel O. (1981), "Un système expert dans le domaine médical", *thèse de 3ᵉ cycle, Université Paris VI*.

[25] Fox J., Rector A. (1982), "Expert systems for medical care?", *Automedica*, vol. 4, pp. 123-130.

17
Expert Systems in
Science and Industry

This chapter gives references to the principal expert systems that have been developed so far for applications in science and industry. The programs are classified according to their fields of application and a few are described in detail.

DENDRAL and META-DENDRAL

The aim of DENDRAL[1] is to identify the structure of an organic molecule, using chemical, physical and spectroscopic data. Interpretation of these data items gives possible structures for fragments of the molecule, and assembly of these fragments then gives possibilities for the complete structure. The process takes place in three stages.

(1). *Generation:* enumeration of all the possibilities, using a program called CONGEN[2] based on, and an improvement of, a combinatorial algorithm conceived by J. Lederberg.
(2). *Planning:* application of constraints to restrict the (possibly very large) search space generated by the first stage.
(3). *Testing and classifying:* further reduction of the number of possibilities to be considered by constructing and applying further constraints, and arranging those that remain in decreasing order of plausibility.

META-DENDRAL[3] is an inductive learning program that can be used to improve and generalize the rules used by DENDRAL and also to generate new rules. It operates on mass-spectrometer data, treating the instrument as a black box whose rules one is trying to discover, that is, the rules that govern the fragmentation of organic molecules. Thus a rule that could be inferred by META-DENDRAL is:

(R): N-C-C-C- → N-C * C-C

meaning that if a molecule contains a nitrogen atom linked to a chain of three carbons, the break will be between the two central carbons.

MACSYMA[4]

This is intended as an aid to solving problems in differential and integral calculus, algebraic equations, vector and matrix algebra etc. It represents the results of one of the biggest efforts ever made in the history of AI, totalling some 50 man-years. The system includes:

— rules for simplifying expressions and establishing the equivalence of two expressions, which are easy to use and to which the user can add others if he wishes; for example,

$\sin (x + \frac{1}{2} \pi) \rightarrow \cos x$
$\sin^2 x + \cos^2 x \rightarrow 1$
$\log (a \times b) \rightarrow \log a + \log b$

— procedures for recognizing algebraic forms, not only at the syntactic level but also at the semantic; thus $3x^2 + 4x - 1$ would be recognized as having the form $ax^2 + bx + c$, but so also would $(x - 1)(x + 1)$;

— heuristic and inferential procedures: thus if the user, by means of the command DECLARE, states that a variable n is integral, MACSYMA will deduce that $\cos(n + \frac{1}{2}) \pi = 0$. The use of an algorithm conceived by Genesereth[5] enables taxonomic-type deductions to be made, properties to be transferred from one entity to another and intersections of sets to be considered.

The program is installed at MIT and can be accessed through the ARPA network; it is written in LISP and has been used by many workers.

Other programs have been written to perform algebraic integration, but using a narrower knowledge base; these include Hearn's REDUCE,[6] a program by Laurière based on SNARK[7] and Mitchell's LEX;[8] the last having the advantage of including learning procedures.

PROSPECTOR[9]

This concerns mineral geology, attacking the following problem: given a geological description of a prospective mining zone, what minerals are most likely to be extracted? The program uses reasoning processes that are independent of the particular subject (here, geology), expressed mainly as partitioned semantic networks, efficiently compiled.[10]

Uncertainties in either the data used or the Bayesian inferences drawn by the program can be indicated. The data can be entered at the start of the session in the form of simple statements in a natural language; these statements are analyzed by a semantic grammar that is interpreted by the analysis program LIFER[11] (see Chapter 7) which has been used to develop several natural-language interfaces with databases. The session is usually interactive and the program may ask for supplementary information. Like all other sophisticated expert systems—relating the term to the state of the art in 1984—PROSPECTOR can explain itself to the user at any stage in the session and after it has reached its conclusions.

Several very useful tools have been developed around PROSPECTOR. One provides two-way translation between the internal (semantic network) form of the information and the near-natural language external form; and KAS[12] (Knowledge Acquisition System) helps the user to create new models or to modify those already existing. In particular, KAS will check that the plausibilities associated with the various events satisfy certain constraints; thus if pl(A) denotes the plausibility of the event A, then if A is a subset of B the relation pl(A) > pl(B) must never hold, because A, being a restriction of B, must satisfy more constraints than B, including those on B itself.

Figure 17.1 shows part of PROSPECTOR's inference network. The two numbers associated with each link represent the degrees of sufficiency (DS) and necessity (DN) respectively. A high value of DS means that the event or observation E is sufficient to establish the hypothesis H—an infinite DS would be equivalent to the assertion $E \rightarrow H$; a small value for DN (DN $\ll$ 1) means that E is necessary to establish H: DN = 0 would be equivalent to $H \rightarrow E$. Thus in this diagram the existence of a "neck" is shown as being strong evidence (DS = 300) of the presence of igneous rocks but not at all necessary (DN = 1); that of "dikes" or "volcanic intrusions" is rather less strong (DS 75 and 20 respectively) but no more necessary. But the fact that a certain volume is characterized by igneous rocks is both necessary and sufficient, and both to a high degree, for it to be classed as an abyssal or bathyal environment.

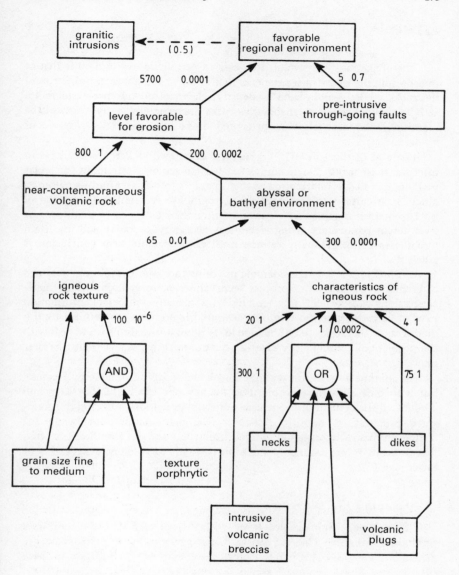

Figure 17.1   Part of the inferential network in PROSPECTOR (*from Duda*[9])

LITHO

One of the most important problems in petroleum exploration is that of interpreting the many measurements that relate to the physical properties of the rocks of the region, such as density, electrical conductivity and radio-activity. Such measures enable the rocks traversed by a test drill to be identified, and are generally presented as curves known as wireline or electrical logs.

The aim of the LITHO[13,14] program, developed at Schlumberger, is to interpret these measurements much as a human geologist would, in particular making use of such information as the geography of the area and its palaeontology, stratigraphy, mineralogy and petrography. A detailed description of the basement is obtained by combining the evidence carried by a hundred or so different parameters, using weights as necessary, tentative and uncertain hypotheses being gradually refined until an acceptably firm conclusion is reached.

LITHO makes very considerable use of methods for combining measures of credibility; this type of process seems inherent in geology, where many conclusions can be held only tentatively, and many sources of information have to be called upon to reinforce an initial hypothesis—sometimes contradicting it, so that it has to be abandoned. It is not unusual to have to deal with the problem of contradictory data; we have something to say about this later on.

An attempt to interpret wireline logs had already been made by Davies[15] but with only a single example used for any one case. LITHO takes into account all those relating to the case under investigation, referring to sound-wave propagation, density, resistivity, gamma-radiation, etc; when the different types of information derived from these are put together it is often found that many are redundant and some contradictory, many sources of error being possible.

Stages in LITHO's reasoning

LITHO was originally developed with the aid of EMYCIN[16] and uses production rules (see Chapter 12) with the same syntax; its conclusions are generally given a weight, which we call the credibility. In addition to these rules it has a broad taxonomic knowledge base on mineralogy, palaeontology, geography, petrography and stratigraphy which enables it to make use of information that is more general than the input data. Thus suppose there is a rule beginning "IF THE GEOLOGICAL PERIOD IS THE SECONDARY AND . . ." but the user enters "THE GEOLOGICAL PERIOD IS THE JURASSIC", the rule will be activated because LITHO "knows" that JURASSIC is part of the SECONDARY. Part of the petrographic tree is shown in Fig. 17.2.

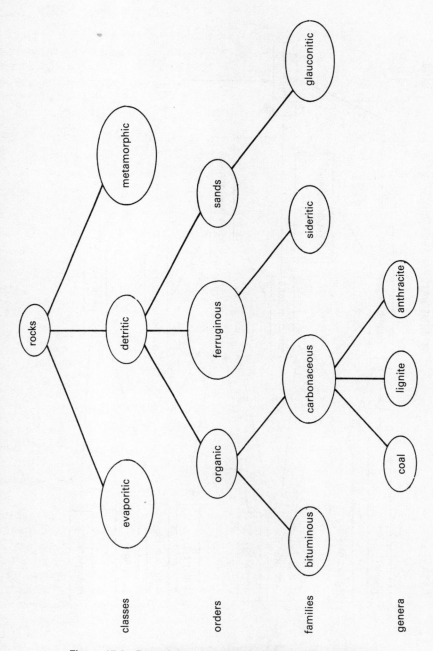

Figure 17.2   Part of the petrographical taxonomy in LITHO

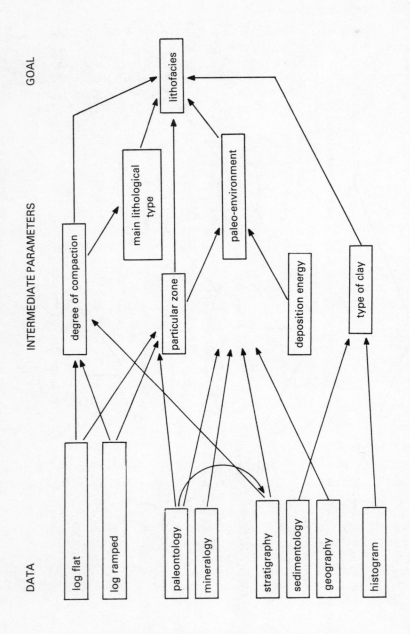

Figure 17.3   Stages in the reasoning

Data from different sources

The main task performed by LITHO is the determination of those rock types, from among the 90 in its knowledge base, that can most plausibly be said to constitute the zone in which the well has been sunk. Figure 17.3 shows the information flow between the data provided and the goal aimed at; a number of intermediate parameters, of the order of 10, are used in the process. The graph of the reasoning process is very broad—many rules converge on a single parameter—but not very deep, the average depth being only 4 levels.

Determination of the broad lithological structure

Detailed identification of rock types is complicated by the fact that many types ("facies") have similar log profiles, silexite cherts and quarzite for example, so that discrimination between the two can only be made by using other geological data. However, some progress can be made by first identifying "super-groups" for later differentiation on the basis of other considerations: saline rocks, dolomitic rocks well compacted or otherwise, heavy rocks (phosphates, siderites, ferruginous limestones, etc); in Fig. 17.3 these occupy the box labelled "histogram".

For example, LITHO's Rule 54 is:

if   percentage of "GYPSUM" in the histogram exceeds 5%
then   the palaeoenvironment of the deposition zone is lagoon (0.7),
        coastal (0.3), reef (0.2), lake (0.2), open sea (−0.95)

External data

The term refers to all the types of information derived from sources other than the logs. Some such items are not always available, such as descriptions of splinters of rock found in the mud during the exploration, or palaeontological items such as indications of the presence of coral. Others are always known or can be inferred: thus valuable information about the types of rock usually encountered in the region can be derived from the knowledge of the geographical location of the well, such as the carbonate platforms of the Middle East. In the majority of cases geographical information will enable a partial deduction of the age of the formations to be made, from which important conclusions can be drawn.

It often happens that LITHO can deduce the geological age from palaeontological information even though the geologist does not know it; for example LITHO knows (as every good geologist should) that (Rule 101) the presence of graptoliths shows that the period is probably either Silurian or Ordovician.

External knowledge can be put into 8 classes, as given below. It consists both of taxonomic structures by means of which data entered into the system can be used to gain access to very general rules, and of inference rules that are activated when data are entered. An example is: if the formation is Cambrian (rocks very old, over 570 million years) then there is a strong probability that the rocks are highly compacted.

The 8 categories are as follows:

geographical (geological regions, basins, fields, wells)
tectonic activities (folds, faults, systems)
stratigraphic (geological era, epoch, system)
palaeontology (fossils)
mineralogy (calcite, quartz)
petrography (limestone, shale, sand)
sedimentology (reefs, channels, meanders, dunes)
petrophysics (porosity, permeability, saturation)

The following is an example of a rule that combines geographical and stratigraphical information.

Rule 295
if   (1)   the stratigraphic period is Cretaceous
and   (2)   the geological formation is one of:
             Iranian platform, Zagros folded belt
then   (1)   probable palaeoenvironments are:
             FLUVIAL (−0.6) LAKE (−0.6) DELTA (−0.6)
             GLACIAL (−0.8) ARID (−0.6) LAGOON (−0.3)
             PELAGIC (0.4) . . .
        (2)   probable principal lithological types for the zone are
             detritic (−0.3) biological (0.3) evaporitic (0.3) plutonic (0.5)
        (3)   there is a small plausibility suggesting that the zone is not
             globally compacted (−0.2)
        (4)   there is a small plausibility suggesting the presence of oil in
             zone (0.2)

The rule below combines the palaeoenvironment of deposition with the principal lithological type to arrive at the most plausible lithofacies.

Rule 201
if   the palaeoenvironment of deposition is NERITIC
and   the principal lithological type is BIOLOGICAL
then the plausibilities of the different lithofacies are:
      HALITE (0.2) DOLOMITE LIMESTONE . . .

Use of the general features of the wireline logs

The logs contain both numerical and symbolic information, and significant features related to the shapes of the curves have important symbolic meanings.

A vocabulary has been developed which helps to describe the log shapes in terms of normalized signatures; typical shapes have been collected and gathered together in a handbook, so that the user can identify them as the program proceeds. All significant symbolic data are compared and contrasted with other data by the LITHO program, thus helping to resolve the question of identification. Figure 17.4 shows two typical traces and Figure 17.5 a third trace together with some of the descriptive features. The main features are:

Plateaux: regions showing a broadly constant response over a distance of at least 25m.

Megaramps: regions of generally steady increase or decrease over a distance of at least 25m.

Major beds: constant response over a distance between 2 and 25m.

Mesoramps: increase or decrease over a distance between 5 and 25m.

A geologist will often talk about a "clay peak" in the gamma-ray trace because high radioactivity is often associated with the presence of clay.

To obtain this information the analyst will ask the user questions about the spontaneous potential curve, that is, the variations of natural voltage with depth, and seek the user's views on the presence of the various features in certain traces, for example those for density, radioactivity and resistivity of the layers. From this data the program calculates the plausibility measures to assign to each of the environments, main lithological groups and perhaps even individual rock types. Any doubts the user may have about the identification of the various features need not hold up this process because he/she is free to qualify his/her views by giving "credibility" factors which the program will use to reduce the strengths of its inferences. An example of the way in which this descriptive information, combined with numerical data, is used is the following rule:

> *Rule 008*
>   if   there is a plateau in the gamma-ray curve
>   and the radioactivity level is below 40API (the international gamma-ray units developed by the American Petroleum Institute)
>   then there is a strong probability (0.8) that the zone is "clean", i.e. has very little clay content.

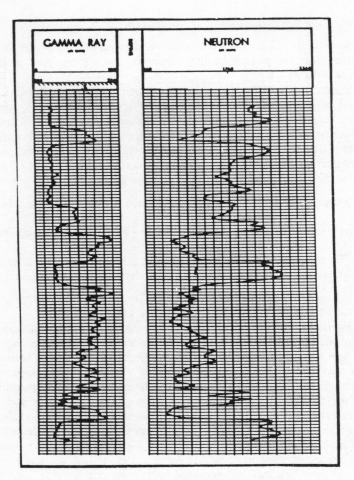

Figure 17.4   Two typical diagraphic traces

Final output from the program

This is produced by a numerically-oriented program that takes into account

— the list of more plausible rock types, together with their credibility factors;
— the logs recorded for the well that is being studied.

The final result from LITHO is a complete geological description of the well at 15cm intervals; experience has shown that this is very close to what a human geologist would produce.

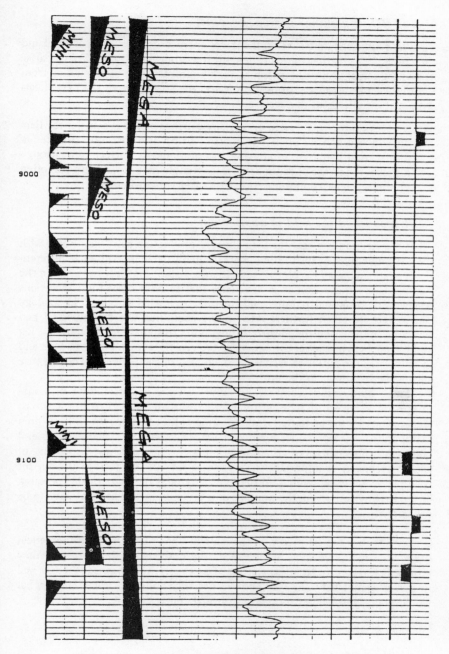

Figure 17.5   The descriptive features of a diagraphic trace

LITHO's handling of erroneous data

The conditions under which the traces are recorded are never optimal and the consequence is that these are seldom free from errors; mistakes can arise also in the actual process of collecting rock fragments, such as one falling from its original place and so being recorded at the wrong depth. LITHO deals with such problems in this way:

— it never claims 100% certainty for any conclusions; so if some of the data on which a conclusion is based prove to be in error, other sources of information may help in arriving at a more nearly correct conclusion;
— it makes much use of redundancies: a strongly-held conclusion will often be the result of combining 5 to 10 weaker conclusions.

Relevance of the field of application

It is a striking fact that the formalism of production rules, combined with the assignment of plausibilities, works equally well in two such different fields as medicine and geology. Actually, the reasoning processes used in the two fields are quite similar in the sense that in both cases the conclusions reached are weak and require confirmation by further checks. The analogy can in fact be taken further: thus in the combined use of numerical and symbolic information the electrocardiogram corresponds to the wireline log and the medical history of the patient to the geological history of the well; and in both cases the aim is to arrive at a diagnosis, of the patient in the one case and of the basement in the other.

These applications contrast strongly with the understanding of visual images or of speech. There, a numerical treatment is applied first (pattern recognition), giving an imperfect description of the phenomenon. This is then manipulated by symbolic methods that call on, for example, general knowledge of the forms of visual images or syntactic – semantic knowledge of speech forms. It is important to appreciate that in the geological case, for example, it is the symbolic information that guides the numerical processing of the logs by restricting the number of individual rock types that have to be considered.

The plausibility measures reflect the experts' assessment of the confidence that can be placed in the conclusions. These have no theoretical basis; they may give some statistical indications but for the most part they represent the accumulated experience of an expert who is asked, "if you had to give a weight between -10 and $+10$ to such-and-such a statement, what would you say?" Thus it is a very informal concept.

Table 17.1

Subject	Theme	Name	Author(s)
Chemistry	Interpretation of mass-spectrograph data	DENDRAL	Feigenbaum[1]
	- ditto - (with learning)	META-DENDRAL	Buchanan[3]
	Organic synthesis	SECS	Wipke[17]
	Organic synthesis	SYNCHEM	Gelernter[18]
Physics	Solution of problems in mechanics	MECHO	Bundy[19]
	Analysis of electrical circuits	SOPHIE	Brown[20]
	Analysis of electrical circuits	PEACE	Dincbas[21]
	Electronics	EL	Brown[22]
	Mechanics		Novak[23]
	Discovery of laws	BACON	Langley[24]
	Resistances of materials	SACON	Bennett[25]
Geology	Mineralogy	PROSPEC-TOR	Duda[9]
	Petroleum	LITHO	Bonnet[13,14]
	Petroleum	DIPMETER ADVISOR	Davis[15]
	Petroleum	DRILLING ADVISOR	Hollander[26]
Mathematics	Discovery of concepts	AM	Lenat[28]
	Integrals, differential equations, etc.	MACSYMA	Moses[4]
	Integrals, differential equations, etc.	REDUCE	Hearn[6]
	Integrals	SNARK/IN-TEGRATION	Laurière[7]
	Integrals (learning methods)	LEX	Mitchell[8]
Computer systems	Sizing VAX configurations	R1, XSEL, XCON,	McDermott[29]
	Fault diagnosis	DART	Bennett[30]
Automatic programming	Program synthesis	PECOS	Barstow[31]
	Program synthesis	DEDALUS	Manna[32]
	Program synthesis	PSI	Green[33]
	Program synthesis	PRO-GRAMMER'S APPRENTICE	Rich[34]
	Program synthesis	SAFE	Balzer[35]
Manufacture	Advice on factory organization	GARI	Descotte[36]
Military	Signal processing	HASP/SIAP	Nii[27]

Existing systems—summing-up

Geological applications have been given pride of place in this account of industrially-oriented systems; this only reflects their position in real life, for they are of major economic importance. Other present-day applications are in agronomy for diagnosis of plant diseases, in biotechnology, in banking for assessment of financial risks, in transport for the maintenance of vehicle fleets, and so on. The greatest commercial success so far has undoubtedly been the suite of programs developed at Digital Equipment Corporation (DEC): the R1 program, and its successor XCON, for configuring VAX machines and XSEL as a sales aid.

The French company Elf-Aquitaine has collaborated with the American AI company Teknowledge in producing an expert system to aid shaft- and well-boring. Also in France CGE is now working on programs to diagnose breakdowns in electrical machinery and CII on systems similar to those of DEC for configuring computers.

Table 17.1 lists the main industrially-oriented systems now in use or in the course of development.

Notes and references

[1] Feigenbaum E., Buchanan B., Lederberg J. (1971), "On generality and problem solving: A case study using the DENDRAL program", in *Machine Intelligence*, Vol. 6, New York, Elsevier.

[2] Carhart R. E. (1979), "CONGEN: An expert system aiding the structural chemist", in *Revolution in the micro-electronic age*, Michie (ed.), Edinburgh, Edinburgh University Press.

[3] Buchanan B., Mitchell T. (1978), "Model-directed learning of production rules", in *Pattern-directed inference systems*, Waterman and Hayes-Roth (eds.), New York, Academic Press.

[4] Moses J. (1967), "A Macsyma primer", *Mathlab Memo 2*, MIT Computer Science Lab.

[5] Genesereth M. (1976), "DB: high-level data base system with inference", *Memo 4*, Macsyma group, MIT.

[6] Hearn A. (1969), *Reduce 2 user's manual*, Stanford AI memo AI-90.

[7] Laurière J. L. (1982), "Utilisation et représentation des connaissances", *RAIRO/TSI*, 1 and 2.

[8] Mitchell T. (1983), "Learning and problem solving", *IJCAI-83*, pp. 1139-1151.

[9] Duda R., Gaschnig J., Hart P. (1979), "Model design in the PROSPECTOR consultant system for mineral exploration", in *Expert systems in the microelectronic age*, D. Michie (ed.), Edinburgh, Edinburgh University Press.

[10] Konolige K. (1979), "An inference net compiler for the PROSPECTOR rule-based consultation system", *IJCAI-79*.

[11] Hendrix G. G. (1977), "Human engineering for applied natural language processing", *IJCAI-77*, pp. 183-191.

[12] Reboh R. (1981), "Knowledge engineering and tools in the Prospector environment", *Techn. Note 243*, Artificial Intelligence Center, SRI International, Menlo Park, California.

[13] Bonnet A., Harry J., Ganascia J. G. (1982), "LITHO, un système expert inférant la géologie du sous-sol", *RAIRO/TSI*, Vol. 1 n° 5, pp. 393-402.

[14] Bonnet A., Dahan C. (1983), "Oil-well data interpretation using expert system and pattern recognition technique", *IJCAI-83*, pp. 185-189.

[15] Davis R., Austin H., Carlbom I., Frawley B., Pruchnik P., Sneiderman R., Gilreath J. A. (1981), "The DIPMETER ADVISOR: interpretation of geologic signals", *ICJAI-81*, Vancouver, pp. 846-849.

[16] Van Melle W. (1980), "A domain-independent system that aids in constructing knowledge-based consultation programs", Stanford University Heuristic Programming Project memo 80-22.

[17] Wipke W. T., Braun H., Smith G., Choplin F., Sieber W. (1977), "SECS-Simulation and Evaluation of Chemical Synthesis: strategy and planning", in W. T. Wipke and W. J. House (eds.), *Computer Assisted Organic Synthesis*, Washington, D.C., American Chemical Society, pp. 97-127.

[18] Gelernter H. L., Sanders A F., Larsen D. L., Agarwal K. K., Boivie R. H., Spritzer G. A., Searleman J. E. (1977), "Empirical Exploration of SYNCHEM", *Science* 197, pp. 1041-1049.

[19] Bundy A., Byrd L., Mellish C., Milne R., Palmer M. (1979), "MECHO, a program to solve mechanics problems", Dept. of A.I. University of Edinburgh, working paper 50.

[20] Brown J. S., Burton R. (1975), "Multiple representations of knowledge for tutorial reasoning", in Bobrow & Collins (eds.), *Representation and understanding*, New York, Academic Press, pp. 311-350.

[21] Dincbas M. (1980), "A knowledge-based expert system for automatic analysis and synthesis in CAD", *Proc. of IFIP Congress*, pp. 705-710.

[22] Brown A., Sussman G. J. (1974), "Localization of failures in radio circuits, a study in causal and teleological reasoning", MIT Artificial Intelligence memo 319.

[23] Novak G. (1977), "Representation of knowledge in a program for solving physics problems", *IJCAI-77*, MIT.

[24] Langley P. (1979), "Rediscovering physics with BACON-3", *IJCAI-79*, Tokyo, pp. 505-507.

[25] Bennett J. S., Engelmore R. (1979), "SACON: a knowledge-based consultant for structural analysis", *IJCAI-79*, pp. 47-49.

[26] Hollander C. R., Iwasaki Y., Courteille J. M., Fabre M. (1983), *Trends and Applications Conference*, Washington.

[27] Nii H. P., Feigenbaum E. A., Anton J. J., Rockmore A. J. (1982), "Signal to symbol transformation: HASP/SIAP case study", the *AI Magazine*, 3, 2, pp. 23-35.

[28] Lenat D. (1980), "On automated scientific theory formation: a case study using the AM program", in Davis & Lenat (eds.), *Knowledge-based systems in Artificial Intelligence*, New York, McGraw-Hill.

[29] McDermott J. (1980), "RI: an expert in the computer systems domains", in *AAAI-80*, pp. 269-271.

[30] Bennett J. S., Hollander C. R. (1981), "DART, an expert system for computer fault diagnosis", *IJCAI-81*.

[31] Barstow D. (1979), *Knowledge-based program construction*, New York, Elsevier.

[32] Manna Z., Waldinger R. (1975), "Knowledge and reasoning in program synthesis", *Artificial Intelligence*, 6, pp. 175-208.

[33] Green C. (1976), "The design of the PSI program synthesis system", *Proc. of the Second International Conference on software engineering*, pp. 4-18.

[34] Rich C., Shrobe H. E. (1976), "Initial report on a Lisp programmer's apprentice", *TR-354*, AI laboratory, MIT, Mass.

[35] Balzer R. M., Goldman N., Wile D. (1977), "Informality in program specification", *IJCAI-77*, pp. 389-397.

[36] Descotte Y., Latombe J. C. (1981), "GARI: a problem solver that plans how to machine mechanical parts", *IJCAI-81*, pp. 766-772.

Part Five

Perspectives for the Future

18
Artificial Intelligence and Computer-Assisted Instruction

Introduction

The subject of this chapter is the use of the computer as an aid to teaching —Computer-Assisted Instruction, CAI. Many programs and systems have been developed along traditional lines for this purpose which have built-in solutions to the problems they put to the pupil, but only very limited powers of reasoning; consequently most of the programs would not be able to solve these problems themselves. The best of the programs do have some abilities for solving problems—where the term is to be understood in its widest sense—but the knowledge base they use is not kept separate from the control mechanisms, so that the combination is difficult to incorporate into the program. For this reason the approach suggested in this chapter is that CAI programs should be organised around expert systems.

In contrast to the traditional systems, Intelligent Computer Assisted Instruction, ICAI, starts from the principle that teaching programs should themselves be expert in the particular field: that is, able to solve the problems they set, possibly in several different ways, and also to follow and to criticize the pupil's solutions. They should also have a theoretical basis for the teaching strategies they use and this should be stated explicitly and not buried in the knowledge base. Further, the strategies should be applicable to several different fields; it is probably unrealistic to hope for some all-encompassing method but it does seem reasonable to expect that some general principles could be laid down. A program with the ability to assess the pupil's knowledge and aptitudes could use these assessments to define a "pupil profile" which could then become one of the parameters used to guide the individual teaching process.

A little history

The usual procedure with CAI is this: first, text material is displayed on the screen of a VDU terminal; then questions are put to the pupil, whose answers must usually be short because the system has little or no power to analyze natural language; finally the program either continues with more difficult material, if the answer is correct, or else indicates the mistakes and their corrections.

Seymour Papert's[1,2] LOGO approach, in the Piaget spirit of spontaneous learning by interaction with the environment, will not be considered here because its aim is less to teach a particular subject than to develop children's creative powers by giving them a device that will react to the ideas they express. With LOGO they can, among other things, create drawings and compose music; the philosophy of this approach is quite the opposite of that of traditional course-instruction programs, which are characterized by a passive attitude on the part of the pupil.

The use of AI techniques in teaching dates from the SCHOLAR[3] program for teaching the geography of South America; as well as having a geographical knowledge base that was more than just prerecorded text this was novel in that either the program or the pupil could take the initiative in the dialog. A later program SOPHIE[4] taught how to find and repair faults in electronic circuits; this had a very resilient natural-language interface with the user that enabled it to understand and to criticize the solutions proposed to it.

Recent research in this field has tended towards the study of the pupils' errors. Use of BUGGY[5] has shown that certain arithmetical errors which at first seemed random were often the consequence of a systematic error in the method used by the pupil. With the educational game WUMPUS[6] the aim is to find the reasons why the players use non-optimal strategies. In parallel with this the programs WHY[7] and GUIDON[8] have made ever more clear the distinction between teaching a particular subject and general strategies for teaching: for example, there is the general rule, "If the pupil does not understand a general rule give him a particular example", which applies whatever the subject. The following paragraphs describe some methods for representing the field to be taught and some of the pedagogical principles that have been developed.

Components of an intelligent CAI system

The last few years' research has resulted in a general schema[9] for a CAI system built around an expert system; this is shown in Fig. 18.1.

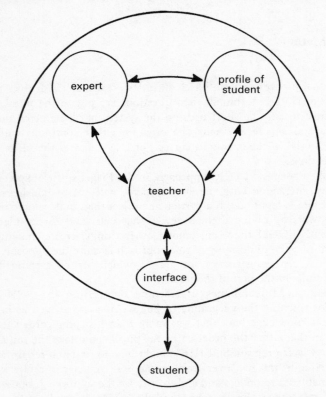

Figure 18.1   Intelligent Computer-Aided Instruction (ICAI)

There is no need to emphasize again the need for a "friendly" interface between the system and the user; but it must be said that technological progress should be taken into account when providing for this communication. This refers particularly to the use of graphical facilities and devices such as "tablets" and "mice" to move the cursor and select items from the screen, which are much quicker and easier to use than methods requiring analysis of natural-language phrases. Research into understanding natural language should of course continue, but in the present state of the art it does not seem to be the most important requirement for the development of CAI. In any case, it is only a question of applying more sophisticated techniques to the field of the teaching program so as to make a deeper understanding possible.

This chapter, therefore, concentrates on two main functions: that of the expert system and that of the teaching system.

The role of the expert system

Whilst the statement made in the introduction to this chapter, that a system intended for teaching a subject should be an expert in that subject, may seem obvious it should not be forgotten that many of the traditional CAI programs cannot themselves solve the problems they put to their pupils: for example, BIP,[10] for teaching BASIC, cannot write a BASIC program although it can correct certain faults in programs submitted to it. Further, an expert program should be able to generate problems, taking into account the parameters of the pedagogical situation such as the pupil's level of attainment, any difficulties expected, how much emphasis to put on a tricky point, the aim of the teaching at any particular moment; and it should be able to deal with a request from the constructor of the type, "Put a problem that is more difficult than the preceding one but which needs the same method of solution".

It should also be able to give well-structured solutions, in which difficult points are made clear and the intermediate steps can be displayed, so that:

— the pupil's solution can be compared with the system's;
— the pupil's method can be assessed, in comparison with the system's;
— help can be given to the pupil who has started on the right track but cannot get beyond a certain step.

The system must be able to combine heuristic and algorithmic methods. The heuristic methods will be acquired from human experts and will have the advantage of being well adapted to explaining methods and difficulties since they show how the human mind works in such situations.[11] The algorithmic methods may have to be used for the sake of efficiency or simply because a sub-problem is too complicated for any other approach; where they do prove unavoidable they should either be supplemented by methods that are more instructive to the pupil or should be treated as a black box—this last is not a rock on which the system founders, for every system, human or otherwise, has some final level beyond which explanation cannot go.

Another requirement is the ability to detect common or systematic mistakes, and if possible to identify any gap in basic understanding that may be the cause of these. This assumes the existence of a non-trivial causal model that can make use of psychological considerations.

Finally, the system must be able to give explanations at a variety of levels. For example, if a chain of inferences a = > b = > c is used in the course of a solution a standard reply to the question, "why c?" is "because b" and a second "why?" gets the response "because a". Actually, the second question often means that the pupil wants to know why b implies c, rather than to go further up the inferential chain. A non-verbal explanation of the Venn diagram type, with sets represented by circles, will often be found very suitable in such cases.

The role of the teaching system

The teacher who is designing the system is the one who must take decisions such as "when is the right moment to give a hint?" or "how far should I let the pupil go along the wrong track?" It is to help deal with such problems that psychological theories can be used as a basis for research into the use of AI in CAI.

The commonly accepted hypothesis is that the pupil has in his mind a model of the knowledge and the skills he is expected to acquire and that he uses this model rigorously in attempting to solve the problems he meets; this implies a deterministic type of behavior on the part of the pupil, driven by the model, and is of course a simplifying assumption. The model is seen by the teacher as a profile of the pupil, which can be used to guide the teaching strategy; in information science terms, values recorded in the profile are passed as arguments to decision functions incorporated into the teaching system. Thus the profile is an approximation made by the teacher to the pupil's internal model, which is only imperfectly known.

The Socratic type of theory of learning propounds the idea that the understanding and learning of complex concepts is helped by the study of special cases from which generalizations can be drawn. Socratic dialog is particularly appropriate for subjects where causal relations enter but do not necessarily apply immediately. This is illustrated by Collins's[8] work. He gives 24 heuristic rules on which to base a discussion leading by progressive steps to the conditions that favor the cultivation of rice. The following is an example of a hypothetical dialog that could be conducted with his system; here T is the teacher and S the student. The relevant rule is given in brackets after each question.

    T: Where is rice grown in North America?
         [Rule 1: ask for a known case]
    S: In Lousiana
    T: Why there?
         [Rule 2: ask for reasons]
    S: Because there's a lot of water there.

T: Right. So do you think there's much rice grown in Washington state or Oregon, for example?
[Rule 6: give a counter-example so as to bring out other necessary factors]

S: No, I don't think so.

T Why not?
[Rule 2: ask for reasons]

S: There's plenty of water but there are also two reasons against growing rice in that area. The climate isn't right and I think the ground isn't flat enough—you have to have flat country so that you can flood it, or at least you have to be able to terrace it.

T: So what about Japan?
[Rule 8: choose a counter-example so as to show what factors are not necessary]
. . ., etc.

One of Collins's heuristics is, "If the student explains a causal relation and includes at least one non-essential factor, look for a counter-example in which this factor has an unfavorable value and ask why the relation does not hold in this case". The knowledge base of his system consists of relations of the type "Water evaporates from the surface of the sea, then the moist air-masses are driven by the winds over the land when they become cooled and so drop their moisture as rain or snow". A fundamental difference from standard course programs is that here a sentence such as this is not a piece of prerecorded text but is derived from a semantic representation held in the system.

The work of Burton and Brown[12] with the game WEST, taken from PLATO,[13] illustrates the "theory of constructive errors". WEST is a board game of "snakes and ladders" type in which traps have to be avoided and advantage taken of short cuts in the progress round a circuit. Each player in turn throws three dice and combines the scores in any way he pleases, using the standard arithmetical operations, to decide how many squares to go forward: the maximum is not necessarily the best choice, and the problem is to find the optimum at each play. As well as being an expert at the game the program has this teaching strategy: whenever it detects a nonoptimal move, it gives a sequence of indications to the player that enable him by degrees to find what his mistake was—for which reason the error is called "constructive". The environment being an educational game, the teacher adopts the principle of not intervening unless there is a significant difference between the pupil's move and the program's.

Carr and Goldstein[14] have developed a theory in which the pupil's internal model is treated as a perturbation of the expert's skills and knowledge. Perturbations can be the result of using incorrect rules; the system must know these incorrect forms and be able to apply them to the problem being studied, so that if the use of a certain incorrect rule gives the same answer as the pupil's, a reasonable assumption is that this forms part of the pupil's mental model. The correct form can then be taught.

These pedagogical theories are as yet very simple and cannot deal with all situations; even so, they represent a stage in the development of non-directive strategies for CAI. The interactive powers of the computer have already been much better exploited in this approach than in the traditional course-instruction programs. And the need for an increasingly clear separation of the particular field of expertise from the general teaching strategies is something that must be kept in mind in all research in this subject.

Architectural constraints on expert systems for CAI

The principle that underlies this section is, "the greatest expert is not necessarily the best teacher". Another expression of this is that the fact that a system can explain *how* it solved a problem and give reasons for choosing one set of assumptions rather than another does not necessarily mean that it can explain *why* it went about things the way it did. The ability to explain the strategies employed implies a degree of detail in the representation of the knowledge that is not essential a priori for the process of solution as such. The concept of compilation is an excellent example of this: the compiled form of a knowledge base or a program is very effective in use but very difficult to understand.

It is generally agreed that modular structure of the representations makes the system's reasoning processes easier to explain. But W. Clancey[15] has commented that the majority of programs jump over intermediate steps in the reasoning, especially when dealing with causal relations, and whilst this does not reduce the efficiency of the process, and may even increase it, it is a disadvantage when the system is required to explain how it reached that particular conclusion. The rule involved here is only a surface manifestation of a deeper phenomenon that has not been represented explicitly.

Conclusion

AI techniques open up new perspectives for pedagogical research. If this opportunity is to be exploited it is essential that expert systems should be made available for teaching purposes, and that they should be as well structured as possible so that they can be used effectively by teaching programs. The computer provides a powerful means for testing theories of learning and of teaching, particularly their generality or, equally, their specificity to one field—and also their effectiveness.[16] Programs that exploit these techniques can explain the steps in their reasoning, instead of simply displaying text on a screen as is done most of the time by the traditional teaching programs.

Notes and references

[1] Papert S. (1970), *Teaching Children Programming*, IFIP Conference on Computer Education, New York, North Holland.

[2] Papert S. (1980), *Mindstorms, Children, Computers and Powerful Ideas*, Basic Books, New York.

[3] Carbonnel J. (1970), "AI in CAI, an artificial intelligence approach to computer-assisted instruction", *IEEE Transactions on man-machine Systems*, Vol. MMS-11, December.

[4] Brown J. S., Burton R. (1975), "Multiple representations of knowledge for tutorial reasoning", in Bobrow & Collins (eds.), *Representation and understanding*, New York, Academic Press.

[5] Brown J. S., Burton R. (1978), "Diagnostic models for procedural bugs in basic mathematical skills", *Cognitive Science 2*, pp. 155-192.

[6] Carr B., Goldstein I. (1977), "Overlays, a theory of modelling for CAI", *MIT AI lab memo 406*.

[7] Clancey W. (1979), "Tutoring rules for guiding a case method dialogue", *International Journal of Man-machine Studies*, 11, pp. 25-49.

[8] Collins A. (1976), 'Processes in acquiring knowledge", in *Schooling and Acquisition of Knowledge*, Anderson, Spiro, Montague (eds.), Hillsdale, N. J., Lawrence Erlbaum Assoc.

[9] Bonnet A., Cordier M. O., Kayser D. (1981), 'An ICAI system for teaching derivatives in mathematics", *Proc. of 3rd World Conference on Computer Education (WCCE)*, Lausanne, 27-31 July.

[10] Barr A., Beard M., Atkinson R. C. (1975), "A rationale and description of a CAI program to teach the BASIC programming language", *Instructional Science*, 4, pp. 1-31.

[11] Polya G. (1945) *How to solve it, a new aspect of mathematical method*, Princeton, Princeton University Press.

[12] Burton R., Brown J. S. (1979), "An investigation of computer coaching for informal learning activities", *IJMMS 11*, pp. 5-24.

[13] Dugdale S., Kibbey D. (1977), "Elementary mathematics with PLATO", Urbana, University of Illinois.

[14] Goldstein I., Papert S. (1977), "Artificial intelligence, language and the study of knowledge", *Cognitive Science*, Vol. 1, 1.

[15] Clancey W., Letsinger R. (1981), "Neomycin: reconfiguring a rule-based expert system for application to teaching", *IJCAI-81*, pp. 829-835, Vancouver.

[16] Stevens A., Collins A., Goldin S. (1979), "Misconceptions in student's understanding", *International Journal of Man-machine Studies*, Vol. 11, pp. 145-156.

19
Programs that can Learn

Introduction

The ability to learn is one of the fundamental constitutents of intelligence, "learning" being understood in its general sense as indicating the way in which humans and animals—and computers—increase their stock of knowledge and improve their skills and reasoning powers.

Study of the learning process has been going on since the early days of AI. For example, Samuel's program CHECKERS[1] held records of a large number of games which it used so as to improve its own play, just as a program written by Waterman[2] learned to play poker: these examples illustrate the point that a program cannot learn effectively unless it has access to a correct representation of the knowledge it is aiming to acquire. Activity in this field declined after a time, largely because other interests, such as methods for representing knowledge, took priority. Now, however, it is flourishing again for the reason that computer programs are being written that are of such a size and such a level of performance that improvement by manual methods is out of the question and that some form of computer-aided improvement process is becoming essential.

Learning had in the past been regarded as being synonymous with adaptation and therefore as consisting in adjusting, by successive approximations, the values of parameters that were believed to characterize the particular structure or concept that was being studied. The aim of such a method is to develop a learning system that becomes increasingly *stable* and increasingly *reliable;* it is close to what is done in pattern classification and recognition.[3] This first type of computer learning was numerical in nature and usually depended on deriving, from the examples provided, some linear or polynomial discriminating function; a good example of this phase is the perceptron (cf. Rosenblatt[4]). The limitations of this approach were soon recognized (cf. Simon[5]) and the main lesson learned was that a learning system that starts without any initial knowledge can never reach a good level of performance.

Learning as understood in AI diverged from this numerical approach during the 1960s and research was directed more towards building symbolic structures based on conceptual relations. An example is the EPAM[6] program of Edward Feigenbaum, which used a discriminating network to study the relations between syllables in experiments on learning by heart. Successive estimation of parameters is often regarded as a method of last resort, required in learning the highest level symbolic structures, but at this period there was not a sufficient understanding of how knowledge could be represented to enable good learning systems to be developed along this new line, and consequently interest declined in the subject in AI circles after the first tentative attempts.

Several types of learning can be distinguished, as follows.

Rote learning and direct incorporation of new knowledge. No powers of inference are required of the program, which simply records the new facts or new examples without applying any transformation; this is the normal style of programming.

Learning by instruction. New items of knowledge or advice are input to the program from outside in a form that can be integrated into the existing stock so as to improve the program's reasoning powers.

Learning by analogy. New facts are acquired that bear a strong resemblance to some already held, with the consequence that the program can adapt its behavior to new situations that have similarities to situations already met.

Learning from examples. To do this a program must infer general rules from particular examples given to it. Thus to teach a program the general concept of "horse" one could give it examples of animals and other objects and tell it which were horses and, possibly, which were not; the program would then have to discover the general rules for recognizing a horse. It is not essential to give negative examples but this speeds up the learning process.

Learning by observation and discovery. This is an unsupervised process that makes the greatest demands on powers of inference. The program examines its own knowledge in an attempt to find regularities from which it can establish new laws and new facts.

Only the last two methods are considered in this chapter; for information on the complete set the reader can consult Michalski, Carbonell, and Mitchell.[7]

General models for learning systems

Among the most general models the one that works along the lines we shall be studying is the two-space model conceived by Simon and Lea.[8] This, shown in Fig. 19.1, consists of an example space and a rule space; it is convenient to use the term "rule", but here the high-level description that has to be inferred from the examples can take a form different from what is usually understood, for example a description that characterizes some object or concept.

An example that will be used frequently in what follows is that of learning the concept of a flush in poker, meaning any five cards all of the same suit e.g., A, K, 9, 4, 2 Spades. From a number of examples the program would

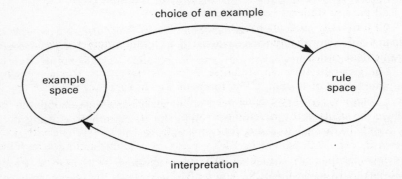

choice of an example

example space

rule space

interpretation

Figure 19.1   Two-space learning model from examples

have to discover that the ranks of the cards were immaterial, that the fact that the suit was, say, Spades, was no criterion since Hearts would do equally, but that the essential property was "all five cards are of the same suit".

The example space. The first necessity for successful learning is good examples that do not contain errors. These examples must be chosen in such a way that they will enable the program to separate the wheat from the chaff—that is, to find the discriminating factors for the concepts that are to be learned. A good learning system should of course succeed in spite of errors in the examples, but at this stage the techniques available are too simple for such a standard to be reached. And in connection with the criterion of discrimination, it would not be sensible to include an ace in every example of a flush given to a program whose task was to deduce the definition of a flush: if it were clever it would detect this regularity and draw the incorrect inference that an ace was an essential component.

A further basic requirement is that the examples should be presented in the right order; this reflects on the teacher of the program, for a good teacher will give examples in increasing order of difficulty.

The rule space. Generalization is the fundamental process involved in learning from examples. A description A is said to be more general than another, B, if A applies in all situations where B applies and also in some others. For example, a generalization of the statement
(1) all chemistry students have bicycles
could be
(2) all science students have bicycles
or
(2′) all students have bicycles.
Rule (2′) could be inferred after other examples had been given, e.g.
(1′) all physics students have bicycles
(1″) all university students have bicycles
which would show that the adjectival part was not important and could therefore be disregarded.

The generalization can of course be wrong; moreover, this is a highly simplified form of learning. The forms of which we are capable are much more complex, for they enable us not only to infer new rules but also to change the structure by which our knowledge is represented.

Another schema expressing functionality is that proposed by Smith[9] and shown in Fig. 19.2; Mitchell's LEX[10] program uses this architecture. This has four components, SELECTION (of problems and examples), PERFORMANCE, ASSESSMENT and LEARNING, with these functions.

PERFORMANCE is the program whose performance is to be improved; it can be a program for playing a game, diagnosing some situation or

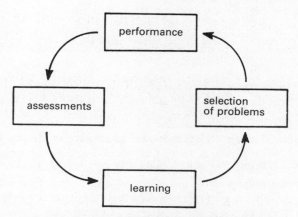

Figure 19.2 Architecture of learning in LEX[10]

developing plans of action for some undertaking that has a stated goal. The assumption is that its performance is not good enough and needs to be improved.

ASSESSMENT is the component that compares the performance achieved with what is expected; the quality of the learning depends of course on the quality of this comparison and therefore on there being an accurate statement of the expected performance. For a medical diagnosis program this will be based on observations of the effects of treatment and of the progress of the illness in many cases of patients who have been treated for this particular illness.

LEARNING is the component that, using the results of the comparison made by ASSESSMENT, decides which constituents of PERFORMANCE are responsible for the less-than-perfect results and which, therefore, need to be changed; these could be either in the knowledge base or in the set of reasoning mechanisms. Of course, improvement for one application could have the retrospective effect of degrading that for a previous one, so a good learning component should review periodically the modifications it has made, to ensure that the overall trend in performance is upwards.

SELECTION is often outside the system, the examples being chosen by hand and input in an order that is optimal for learning; but one can envisage an arrangement in which the system itself decides which examples should be worked on in order to achieve the desired performance.

We will now consider the rules for generalization that are most commonly used.

General rules for induction

In the following, "&" is used to denote the logical product or conjunction and ":: >" for the relation of implication between the description of a concept and its name: thus A:: >B means that B is the name of the concept described by A.

Replacement of constants by a variable. This first rule can be illustrated by the aim to define the concept of a flush in poker. If C1 – C5 are five cards, the predicates SUIT, RANK are used with the notation:

SUIT (C_i, S) means "C_i is a Spade" (similarly for Hearts, Diamonds, Clubs)
Rank $(C_i, 5)$ means "C_i is a 5" (similarly 2 – 10, J, Q, K, A)

Given the two examples

E1: SUIT (C1, S) & SUIT (C2, S) & SUIT (C3, S) & SUIT (C4, S) & SUIT C5, S)
:: > FLUSH (C1, C2, C3, C4, C5)

E2: SUIT (C1, C) & SUIT (C2, C) & SUIT (C3, C) & SUIT (C4, C) &
SUIT (C5, C)
:: > FLUSH (C1, C2, C3, C4, C5)

the program could infer the rule

R1: SUIT (C1, x) & SUIT (C2, x) & SUIT (C3, x) & SUIT (C4, x)
& SUIT (C5, x)
:: > FLUSH (C1, C2, C3, C4, C5)

by replacing the constants S, C by the variable x.

Disregarding conditions. Another method is to disregard one of the conditions included in a rule; the resulting rule will be more general than the original because it can be applied under wider conditions. This strategy can be applied to the following example by ignoring all conditions involving the rank of the cards. Using also the rule of replacing constants by a variable we have

E3: SUIT (C1, S) & RANK (C1, 2) &
SUIT (C2, S) & RANK (C2, 5) &
SUIT (C3, S) & RANK (C3, 7) &
SUIT (C4, S) & RANK (C4, 8) &
SUIT (C5, S) & RANK (C5, K)
:: > FLUSH (C1, C2, C3, C4, C5)
which also generalizes to R1.

Generalization by disjunction. A third method is to add options to the rule, with the disjunction OR; like the preceding method, this widens the conditions and so generalizes the rule.

Suppose we want to teach the meaning of HONOR in Bridge; given the examples

E4: RANK (X, 10) :: > HONOR (X)
E5: RANK (X, J) :: > HONOR (X)
E6: RANK (X, Q) :: > HONOR (X)
E7: RANK (X, K) :: > HONOR (X)
E8: RANK (X, A) :: > HONOR (X)

generalization by disjunction gives the rule

R2: RANK (X, 10) OR RANK (X, J) OR RANK (X, Q) OR RANK (X,
K) OR RANK (X, A)
:: > HONOR (X)

This is in fact a much less risky generalization than the preceding ones.

Generalization by interval. Suppose that we have two examples of members of a class which we are studying and that these are characterized by measures a and $b;$ a reasonable generalization is the assumption that all members of the class have corresponding measures lying between a and b. Clearly, the risk of error decreases as the number of examples increases.

Generalization by tree climbing. The tree of Fig. 19.3 structures the shapes of plane figures; suppose we are given the information

FORM (X, rectangle)   :: >   BLUE (X)
FORM (X, triangle)   :: >   BLUE (X)

then by climbing the tree we get the generalization

FORM (X, polygon)   :: >   BLUE (X)

In other words, if we know that all the members of a class X which are either triangular or rectangular are BLUE, we infer that all polygonal members of X are BLUE.

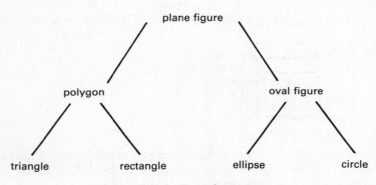

Figure 19.3   Tree of concepts

Winston program

Another well-known example is the program written by Patrick Winston[11] at MIT, to teach the concept of an arch. Figure 19.4 shows how the learning is guided by a suitably chosen sequence of examples. The first picture is a correct example; the second is a "near miss"—an important idea introduced by Winston to indicate that only one of the essential conditions is unfulfilled, in this example the condition that the horizontal block should be supported by the two verticals; the third is also a "near miss" because the two verticals should not touch each other; and finally the fourth picture shows that the horizontal component does not have to be rectangular but can be any prism. The program learns to refine its initial concept of what an arch should be by progressively eliminating the non-essential characteristics from the definition.

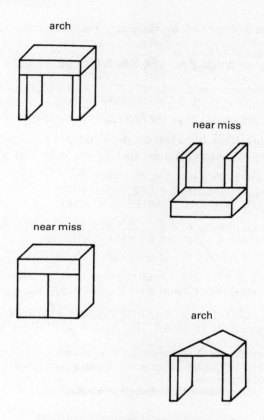

Figure 19.4   Learning the concept "arch"

Learning abstract structures

Dietterich and Michalski's program INDUCE[12] aims to characterize situations or concepts that have some internal structure. In the following figure the components are related to one another in ways that can be described by terms such as ABOVE and BELOW, and the program will try to find the most specific description that generalizes the given examples.

E1:	⬭ ⬭	∃ (u, v): LARGE (u) & CIRCLE (u) & LARGE (v) & CIRCLE (v) & ABOVE (u, v)
E2:	○ ▢ ▢	∃ (w, x, y): SMALL (w) & CIRCLE (w) & LARGE (x) & SQUARE (x) & LARGE (y) & SQUARE (y) & ABOVE (w, x) & ABOVE (x, y)

The program will generate the following structures:

E1': ∃ (u, v): ABOVE (u, v)
E2': ∃ (w, x, y): ABOVE (w, x) & ABOVE (x, y)

from which it deduces that C = ABOVE (u, v) provides the most specific generalization whilst maintaining consistency with the examples.
The representation can be in the form of a syntactic vector:

< SIZE (u), SHAPE (u), SIZE (v), SHAPE (v) >

in terms of which the above examples are

E1': (LARGE, CIRCLE, LARGE, CIRCLE)
E2'': (SMALL, CIRCLE, LARGE, SQUARE)
E2''' (LARGE, SQUARE, LARGE, SQUARE)

from which, by comparing first E1'' and E2'' and the E1'' and E2''', the minimum-generalization algorithm finds the descriptions

(*, CIRCLE, LARGE, *) and (LARGE, * LARGE, *)

where * indicates that the corresponding property is not important.
Using the structural relation again gives the following:

C1: ∃ (u, v): ABOVE (u, v) & CIRCLE (u) & LARGE (v)
C2: ∃ (u, v): ABOVE (u, v) & LARGE (u) & LARGE (v)

which says in words: there is something large above something large and a circle above something large. This could provide a good answer to a question posed as a test of observation.
Other work along these lines is described by Kodratoff.[13]

The AQ11 program

The next method to be described provides an alternative to the more traditional method of formulating decision rules by conducting long discussions with a human expert in the field. Although the human expert has made the right decision in many cases he often has difficulty in explaining just how he has gone about this, forgetting to mention certain parameters (which he takes into account almost subconsciously), and in giving any precise assessment of the strength of the conclusions he draws.

The alternative given here is to code the information contained in known examples in a form that can be used by a learning program; and the simplest way is to represent the examples by the same syntactic forms as will be used for the rules that are to be discovered.

The AQ11 program was developed by Ryszard Michalski[14] of the University of Illinois and used to develop rules for diagnosing diseases of soya.[15] The known examples were descriptions of 630 diseased plants, expressed as sets of parameter/value pairs together with the known diagnosis: the number of possible diagnoses was 15 and as there were 35 parameters, each able to take between 2 and 7 values, the number of possible symptoms was of the order of 10.[15]

Here is an example of a rule given by the expert:

if   leaves are normal & stalk abnormal
    & collar is cankered
    & stalk is cankered, color brown
then root has rot caused by a rhizoctonia.

The program's algorithm transforms the problem of discovering discriminating rules into one of learning a series of concepts. It first considers all the positive examples that belong to a certain class or have a certain diagnosis and constructs a description that is sufficiently general to include them all. It then restricts this description so as to exclude all the negative examples (meaning all those that are included in other classes), and so on for each class in turn. The program chooses first the most "interesting" examples, that is, those that are most widely separated in the sample space; thus in this application it chose a sample of 290 plants for the learning process, leaving the remaining 340 to be used to test the rules derived from the 290.

This learning process leads to an expert-system program; let us call this PL, and the corresponding program constructed by the classical method of discussions with human experts PD. In the case of this application of AQ11 the human expert proposed some descriptions that required more detail than was required by the AQ11 formalism, such as rules in which certain properties played an essential role whilst others were used only for confirmation. In spite of this greater flexibility PD was found to be less effective than PL, the latter giving the correct diagnosis in 97.6% of the tests against 71.8% for PD; further, on 100% of occasions PA gave a shortlist within which the correct diagnosis was contained, against 96.9% for PD, and the PL list was also shorter and therefore could be acted on with less risk of error.

It would not however be justifiable to take the results of this experiment as proof that expert systems constructed by such a learning process are systematically superior to those based on discussion with experts. For one thing, in this application there was a direct correspondence between symptoms and diagnoses; the learning program would deal much less well with a situation in which intermediate conclusions had to be used, or strategies that depended on the conclusions. For another, the syntactic forms generated by the program are limited in scope; the human expert uses other forms of reasoning than production rules, and even with production rules he uses several forms, some leading to a possible diagnosis and others serving to confirm this: it would be difficult to achieve this distinction by means of a learning program.

Some of the rules generated by PL are overburdened with logic and can be simplified, but the program does not have the commonsense machinery to enable it to make the simplifications. Even so the achievement is striking, and the technique could be applied in other, similar, fields. Most of the rules have been commended by experts; overall, it seems that this use of learning methods should be viewed as an aid to the expert in producing his rules, and so as a new way in which the information scientist can cooperate with the subject specialist.

The AM program

This was produced by Douglas Lenat[16] at Stanford; it is a spectacular example of a program that generates concepts by using heuristics that are very similar to those used by learning programs. AM is not a learning program in the sense previously defined because it does not use new knowledge to improve its performance; instead, it modifies its activities in the light of its discoveries. It is included here because it has all the potential of a learning program.

AM starts with a knowledge base of 115 concepts belonging to set theory and represented as structured objects (cf., Ch. 13); in addition it has a number of heuristics expressed as production rules, which can be applied to these initial objects so as to create new ones.

Objects in AM Every object has a standard set of properties; these are DEFINITION, EXAMPLES and COUNTER-EXAMPLES, GENERAL-IZATIONS, SPECIALIZATIONS. There is also WORTH, a numerical indication of the interest or importance of the concept. Consider as an example the object "prime numbers":

> NAME: Prime numbers
> DEFINITIONS:
>   ORIGIN: number-of-divisors-of $(x) = 2$
>   PREDICATE-CALCULUS: prime $(x) = (\forall y) (y \mid x) = > y = 1$ or
> $y = x$ (exclusive)
> EXAMPLES: 2, 3, 5, 7, 11, 13, 23
> GENERALIZATIONS:
>   integers
>   integers having an even number of divisors
> SPECIALIZATIONS:
>   even primes
>   odd primes
>   prime pairs
>   . . .
> WORTH: 800 (see H2 below)

The following four heuristic rules are used frequently by AM; they enable us to see just how the program goes about finding new concepts.

H1: IF specializations of a concept C have been generated AND IF the current task is to find examples of each of these THEN consider the known examples of C; these may also be examples of some of the new specialized concepts.

H2: IF it is found that all the examples of a concept C are examples of another concept D AND IF it is not already known that C is a specialization of D THEN make the assumption that C is a specialization of D AND increase WORTH for the two concepts.

H3: IF all the examples of a concept are included in the domain of definition of a seldom-used function THEN compute the image of these elements under the function AND study the resulting set as a separate concept.

H4: IF a concept is found to have very few examples THEN try to find why AND consider the concept as having little interest.

If H1 is applied to the integers $1 - 1000$ and to the concept of having a stated number of divisors the result is

D_0 = numbers with 0 divisors: none
D_1 = numbers with 1 divisor: 1
D_2 = numbers with 2 divisors: 2, 3, 5, 7, 11, 13, . . .
D_3 = numbers with 3 divisors: 4, 9, 25, 49, 121, 169, . . .

H4 suggests that very small sets are of no interest, so D_0 and D_1 can be eliminated. No heuristic applies to D_2 but D_3 are perfect squares; H3 recommends considering their square roots, which prove to be the set D_2, the primes. By H2, therefore, their WORTH should be increased.

Thus AM generates new concepts by applying its heuristics to existing concepts. It cannot, of course, create new heuristics, and this is a serious limitation from the point of view of a learning program. Learning always takes place at a level above that of procedures; an ability to discover new heuristics implies the existence of meta-heuristics to manipulate the heuristics, which in turn implies the existence of meta-meta-heuristics, and so on.

The BACON-3 program

BACON-3[17] is a program that (re-)discovers empirical laws, in particular certain laws of physics such as the perfect gas laws, Coulomb's law, Ohm's law or Gallileo's law. It does this by using heuristics to detect regularities in data given to it, from which it formulates hypotheses which it then seeks to check.

A useful heuristic for detecting the existence of a relation between two numerical variables is:

> IF the values of a variable V1 increase when the values of another variable V2 increase THEN assume a monotone increasing relation between V1 and V2 AND calculate the slope.

Given the data of Fig. 19.5 the program rediscovers the gas law

PV = nRT

It proceeds in stages. First it observes that as P increases V decreases, which leads it to consider the product PV; this is found not to be constant, but it does keep the same value when T remains constant. Since PV is found to increase with T the program considers PV/T, the values of which are given in Fig. 19.6. The next observation is that this last quantity increases with the number of moles, *n*, of the gas, suggesting consideration of a new quotient PV/nT; and this, as shown in Fig. 19.7, is found to be constant. In the course of its search the program will have considered other possibilities and found that they did not lead to an interesting result.

Moles	*Temperature*	*Pressure*	*Volume*	*PV*
1	300	300 000	0,008 320 0	2 496.0
1	300	400 000	0,006 240 0	2 496.0
1	300	500 000	0,004 992 0	2 496.0
1	310	300 000	0,008 597 3	2 579.2
1	310	400 000	0,006 448 0	2 579.2
1	310	500 000	0,005 158 4	2 579.2
1	320	300 000	0,008 874 7	2 662.4
1	320	400 000	0,006 656 0	2 662.4
1	320	500 000	0,005 324 8	2 662.4

Figure 19.5   Data satisfying the perfect gas laws

Moles	*Temperature*	*PV*	*PV/T*
1	300	2 496.0	8.32
1	310	2 579.2	8.32
1	320	2 662.4	8.32
2	300	4 992.0	16.64
2	310	5 158.4	16.64
2	320	5 324.8	16.64
3	300	7 488.0	24.96
3	310	7 737.6	24.96
3	320	7 987.2	24.96

Figure 19.6   Values obtained from Fig. 19.5 after deciding that PV/T might be an interesting quantity

Moles	PV/T	PV/NT
1	8.32	8.32
2	16.64	8.32
3	24.96	8.32

Figure 19.7   Values obtained from Fig. 19.6 after deciding that PV/NT, where N is the number of moles of the gas, might be an interesting quantity

Conclusion

The learning techniques developed so far are still very specialized, because they are either confined to restricted domains or dependent on knowledge structures that are limited by a rigid syntax; in contrast, our own learning methods vary according to the subject and can function in the most varied fields. Very few existing programs have real learning abilities; their stock of knowledge is increased by human intervention after human assessment of their performance. But this will become more and more difficult in future, with the production of programs having millions, perhaps tens or even hundreds of millions, of rules. Learning programs have indeed a great future before them.

Notes and references

[1] Samuel A. L. (1963), "Some studies in machine learning using the game of checkers", in *Computers and thought*, Feigenbaum and Feldman (eds.), New York, McGraw-Hill, pp. 71-105.

[2] Waterman D. A. (1970), "Generalization learning techniques for automating the learning of heuristics", *Journal of Artificial Intelligence 1*, pp. 121-170.

[3] Selfridge O. G., Neisser U. (1963), "Pattern recognition by machine", in *Computers and thought*, Feigenbaum and Feldman (eds.), New York, McGraw-Hill, pp. 237-256.

[4] Rosenblatt, F. (1958), "The perceptron: a theory of statistical separability in cognitive systems", *Technical Report VG-1196-G-2*, Cornell aeronautical lab.
The perceptron is a system for the classification of objects in which the criteria for distinguishing between the classes are derived as linear functions of the characteristics of the objects.

[5] Simon H. (1983), "Why should machines learn", in *Machine learning, an artificial intelligence approach*, Michalski, Carbonell and Mitchell (eds.), Palo Alto, California, Tioga Publishing Company.

[6] Feigenbaum E. A. (1963), "The simulation of verbal learning behavior", in *Computers and thought*, Feigenbaum and Feldman (eds.), New York, McGraw-Hill, pp. 228-284.

[7] Michalski R. S., Carbonell J. G., Mitchell T. M. (1983) eds., *Machine learning, an artificial intelligence approach,* Palo Alto, California, Tioga Publishing Company.

[8] Simon H. A., Lea G. (1974), "Problem solving and rule induction: a unified view", in L. Gregg (ed.), *Knowledge and Acquisition,* Hillsdale, N.J., Lawrence Erlbaum.

[9] Smith R. G., Mitchell T. M., Chestek R. A., Buchanan B. G. (1977), "A model for learning systems", Stanford Heuristic Programming Project Memo HPP-77-14.

[10] Mitchell T. M. (1983), "Learning and problem solving", *IJCAI-1983,* pp. 1139-1151.

[11] Winston P. H. (1975), "Learning structural descriptions from examples", in *The psychology of computer vision,* P. Winston (ed.), New York, Mc-Graw-Hill, 1975.

[12] Dietterich T. G., Michalski R. S. (1981), "Inductive learning of structural descriptions: Evaluation criteria and comparative review of selected methods", *Artificial Intelligence 16,* pp. 257-294.

[13] Kodratoff Y., Sallantin J. (1983), eds. "Outils pour l'apprentissage", *Publications du GR 22,* Journées d'Orsay, January, 1983.

[14] Michalski R. S., and Larson J. B. (1978), "Selection of most representative training examples and incremental generation of VL1 hypotheses: The underlying methodology and the description of programs ESEL and AQ11", *Rep. No. 867,* Computer Science Dept., University of Illinois, Urbana.

[15] Michalski R. S. and Chilausky R. L., "Learning by being told and learning from examples: An experimental comparison of the two methods of knowledge acquisition in the context of developing an expert system for soybean disease diagnostic", *International Journal of Policy Analysis and Information System 4,* pp. 125-161.

[16] Lenat D. B. (1977), "The ubiquity of discovery", *Artificial Intelligence,* Vol. 9, 3.

[17] Langley P. (1981), "Data-driven discovery of physical laws", *Cognitive Science 5,* 31-54.

20
Promise and
Performance

The aim of this final chapter is to give an idea of what successful applications of artificial intelligence can be expected in the reasonably near future and what are likely to remain subjects for research for some years to come. In most fields such attempts at prediction have revealed gross errors in appreciation of what can be expected in the short term and this one certainly runs the same risks; but the results do at least agree broadly with estimates made recently by American[1] and European[2,3] research workers in response to the announcement of the Japanese Fifth Generation project. The predictions are confined to the two subjects on which the main emphasis has been placed in this book, expert systems and the understanding of natural languages.

In the present state of technology the attempt to make the computer understand completely unrestricted natural language runs up against intractable problems. The fact that the program has no contact with the real, external world, being unable for example to see and to know who is speaking or to find out enough about the physical environment to be able to separate the information signal from any noise that may be degrading its quality, makes it necessary for present-day designers to base their programs on simplifying assumptions. These will include such assumptions as that speech is presented as isolated words (the speaker making a distinct break between each word and the next), both the vocabulary and the syntax are restricted and the number of speakers is very small, usually only one.

The current commercial systems are restricted to a single speaker and a few hundred words, which must be spoken distinctly with a short pause after each one; there are also programs that enable robots to be controlled by spoken commands. More elaborate systems, such as the IBM system which can understand several thousand words, do not work in real time because the time needed for the computation is too great: this particular program uses methods that depend on the probabilities of certain words being followed by certain others, a method which is not used by human hearers.

So understanding of speech outside a very restricted field remains a long-term objective; it will have to draw on the results of research into machine understanding of written language (i.e. language typed on a terminal's keyboard), which has already gone a good deal further because it is not hindered, as speech is, by loss of information resulting from incomplete interpretation of the signal. Information lost in this way is often irretrievable, even with the aid of knowledge at the semantic or pragmatic level. Such short-term progress as can be expected will result from specialized chips being developed for particular tasks; with these, analysis can be carried on in parallel at different levels, dealing for example with word selection and syntactic, semantic and pragmatic aspects, each contributing to a program that attempts to resolve any conflicts and then to arrive at the most probable interpretation.

Over the next few years the market will be flooded with systems for extracting information from databases in response to natural-language queries; and research will continue, with the aim of providing systems that respond more intelligently and cooperate more closely with the user, taking into account in particular the general rules of dialog, the motivation and possibly also the profile of the user. The machine will then be able to vary the nature of its reply according to what it knows of the user. Further, the machine will not be restricted to drawing only on its knowledge base for the subject of a query but will have resources of "commonsense" to help it conduct very general reasonings and thus display more intelligent behavior: but this is for the very long term.

Understanding and generation of documents is still in a very primitive state; searching of documents, by its very nature, requires an unlimited vocabulary and present methods can do no more than identify keywords. Future progress in understanding natural language should make it possible for the machine to discern more precisely what it is that the enquirer wants and to find the relevant references, instead of giving a long list of possibilities for him to look through. Automatic production, or at least automatic aid to production, of highly specialized manuals such as for repair or maintenance of machinery is likely to become possible within the next five years.

Expert systems have already proved successful, both on the technical level and as reservoirs of expertise. On the technical level, they will in the future replace many traditionally-written, that is, algorithmic, programs that have become too large to update or improve. As reservoirs of expertise, it is likely that many small-scale systems, say having a few hundred rules, will be developed as an aid to dealing with very specialized problems for which human experts exist but are not easily available. In some cases the expertise that is vital to some undertaking or some company is confined to a handful of specialists whose loss or departure would be disastrous; in such cases it becomes a matter of major importance, on both economic and scientific grounds, to capture this expertise in programs that are easily and widely accessible. As well as being safeguarded, it can then be discussed, questioned and brought up to date as new knowledge becomes available.

Developments in the following fields can be expected: banking, for risk assessment, bankruptcy matters, investment advice; insurance, for providing a pool of general expertise and for setting premiums; legal and administrative affairs, for providing advice and help in connection with such matters as sale of property, inheritance. Whether the program is dealing with professionals who know and understand the technical vocabulary or with members of the general public who simply use microcomputers at home, the level of expertise will vary accordingly. There will also be applications in the event of natural catastrophes such as floods, landslides, volcanic eruptions, earthquakes, fires, etc. where control of the situation or advice can be provided by expert systems that will keep their heads and work efficiently and tirelessly to organize the rescue measures.

Research will continue, with the aim of producing systems having tens of thousands of rules. This will require new architectures to be developed; in particular parallel processing will be essential, both at the hardware and the software level. These systems will have several levels of knowledge, the higher levels making possible a more intelligent use of the lower: if a program is asked for the telephone number of someone who has died it should not have to search its database to see if it has this number.

Different systems concerned with the same subject, for example medicine or agriculture, will be linked by wide-area telecommunication networks so that one can pass on a question to another if it considers the second to be better equipped to answer that particular question; this could be so with medical queries, for example. For agriculture, there could be specialized systems for each region of a country; thus for France a system for the south west could specialize in grapes, for the Vaucluse in melons and so on.

Expert systems will make it easier to transfer know-how between different fields and to question their knowledge items and methods of reasoning; they will also serve as bases for discussion between experts in the same or different fields who may not use the same methods in attacking problems. When applied to computer-aided teaching they will be able to show the learner the steps in the argument instead of simply displaying text on the screen as is done by the present teaching programs. In fact, if the computer's capacities for reasoning and for interaction are not to be exploited, it seems better to stay with that more traditional (and more portable) aid to learning, the book.

Present-day methods for representing knowledge are still limited to certain types of task. Diagnostic problems are the best understood, generally consisting in finding an hypothesis (which will be called the diagnosis) that explains, in a consistent manner, a set of data. Problems of prognosis or of construction of a complex structured object such as a building are still a long way from satisfactory solution, especially when the descriptive parameters cannot be expressed in the technical vocabulary, as for example when there are aesthetic criteria to be considered. Some types of information, such as spatial or temporal relations, are given in an ad hoc fashion for particular problems and do not generalize readily. With our prsent resources we have to represent spatial information in the machine by explicit statements that replace our physical perception of space; it is unlikely that we shall be able to link means for aural or visual perception to expert systems on any significant scale within the next five years.

Tools for building expert systems, usually called "shells", will continue to be developed and will enable new ranges of problems to be attacked; these will help in making use of knowledge from different fields, provided that it can be expressed in each case in similar syntaxes and that the aims are similar. The symbiotic relationship with research in understanding natural language will lead to systems that are more and more easily usable by people who are not information-science specialists; and programs will be developed for the specialized task of extracting from surrounding material the essential knowledge to be used by the cognitive scientist in his combined logical and psychological work of helping the human expert to pass on his complete stock of knowledge and to structure it in a way that can be used by inferential mechanisms.

For lack of any better way, information scientists today continue to improve the knowledge bases of their programs by hand. The small size of the existing programs makes this acceptable, but what will happen when they get to the size of a million rules or concepts? Programs on this scale will themselves have to learn from experience and to improve themselves by using simple rules provided by human experts for assessing their performance. First they will become able to improve their knowledge bases, and after that their mechanisms for using this knowledge, that is, their higher level strategies. The standard criticism that computers can do only what they have been told to do will become less and less justified.

Notes and references

[1] Feigenbaum, E. A., McCorduck, P. (1983), *The Fifth Generation*, Reading, Mass. Addison-Wesley (London, Pan Books 1984).
[2] Project ESPRIT (1983), Report of the EEC, Brussels.
[3] English, M. (1983), "The European IT-Industry", Report of the EEC, Brussels.

Glossary

The following are some of the important AI and information science terms used in this book.

Algorithm	Step-by-step description of the solution of a problem. Becomes a program when written in a programming language.
Blackboard model	Model of a reasoning process in which the different parts of the system communicate with each other through the intermediary of a structure called "blackboard".
Control structure	Strategy for reasoning, allowing the knowledge relevant to a subject to be used in solving a problem in that subject.
Database	Set of facts relevant to a particular subject.
Data structure	The organization of set of data: vectors, arrays, lists, etc.
Frame	A structure that represents a standard object.
Heuristics	Informal rules for reasoning; defined by Polya as "the art of guessing right".
Inference engine	*See* Control structure.
Instantiation	Replacement of a variable in an expression by a constant. Also, a process by which a specific example of an abstract concept is created; the instantiated object has all the general properties of the abstract object and may have other properties peculiar to itself.
Knowledge base	That part of an expert system that contains the facts and the valid inferences relevant to its subject.
LISP	The most popular AI language.
Pattern matching	Process by which agreement is found between a given situation and a set of criteria that characterize a standard situation; e.g., a natural-language sentence compared with a grammar, a set of symptoms compared with an illness. The agreement is often only partial.
Predicate	A function of one or more arguments, returning a value TRUE or FALSE.

Production rule   A situation/action pair.
PROLOG   The second most popular language in AI.
Symbolic   Representation of concrete objects by abstract forms.
representation
System   In contrast to its use in "system theory", used here as synonymous with "program".

Abbreviations

AAAI	American Association for Artificial Intelligence
AFCET	Association Française de Cybernétique et d'Études Techniques
CACM	Communications of the Association for Computing Machinery
CAD	Computer-Assisted Design
CAI	Computer-Assisted Instruction
COLING	Conference on Computational Linguistics
IEEE	Institute for Electrical and Electronic Engineers
IFIP	International Federation of Information Processing
IJCAI-83	8th International Joint Conference on Artificial Intelligence, Karlsruhe, West Germany, 1983
IJCAI-81	7th, Vancouver, Canada, 1981
IJCAI-79	6th, Tokyo, Japan, 1979
IJCAI-77	5th, MIT, Cambridge, Mass., USA, 1977
IJCAI-75	4th Tbilisi, USSR, 1975
RAIRO/TSI	Revue d'Automatique Informatique et Recherche Opérationnelle - Techniques et Science Informatiques
TINLAP	Theoretical Issues on Natural Language Processing

Index

(The names of programs are in capitals)

219